An Island to Myself

"In this inspiring and hope-filled journey into the heart of solitude, McGregor takes us to the hinterlands of grace, and in the healing silence of a still heart and mind, we discover the antidote to a loneliness that plagues many of us these days, fed by consumption, competition, and a tendency to commodify relationships." —**Patrick Hannon**, author of *Sacrament: Personal Encounters with Memories, Wounds, Dreams, and Unruly Hearts*

"To dwell in solitude without feeling lonely, one must be open to a presence that's inaccessible in the midst of even the dearest human companions. In search of that elusive presence, Michael N. McGregor has repeatedly taken leave from loved ones and workaday tasks, seeking stillness in a library, a park, a rustic cabin, a borrowed apartment, a Greek island, and other retreats. Over the course of decades, from restless youth to grateful elder, he has gathered insights into his character, his values, his past and possible futures. By accompanying him in his search, we may be inspired to undertake solitary sojourns of our own." —**Scott Russell Sanders**, author of *The Way of Imagination*

"Solitude is one of the most misunderstood words in the English language. Many of us would prefer to avoid being alone. But when we allow solitude to take us by the hand, we realize it is a guide, a doorway we step through to discover the most consequential person in our life: our self. As we follow along in this page-turner of a book—from the Greek island of Patmos to the San Juan Islands, Whidbey Island, and a myriad of other places McGregor has experienced solitude—we start to understand that being still is also a way to keep moving, to keep going deeper into the discovery of our true purpose and being." —**Judith Valente**, former faith and values correspondent for PBS-TV, author of *The Art of Pausing* and *How to Be*

"I finished *An Island to Myself* within the whirlwind of my screen-mediated over-extended life, one where my harried attention leaps quickly here then there and back again. Yet McGregor's book is not finished with me. Its steady openhearted questions about fulfillment, gratitude, beauty, love, and meaning still call to me from within. His patient and humble account of the difficulties and rewards of seeking solitude, not in order to be alone and separate, but ultimately to love and connect more fully and more deeply with life, is one I won't soon forget." —**David Naimon**, co-author of *Ursula K. Le Guin: Conversations On Writing*, and host of the radio show and podcast, Between The Covers

"Michael N. McGregor's forty-year courtship of solitude is exacting, frank about the paradoxes of the journey, utterly determined to see his investigation through, and faithful to a helpful decision to include the journey's contradictions. Bolstered by a counterpoint of epigraphs on solitude ranging from Wordsworth to Einstein, Epictetus to Proust, Anne Frank to Susan Sontag, Joan Didion to Rumi, Franz Kafka to bell hooks, and more, journey's end brings McGregor to conclusions that are thoroughly flight-tested, uniquely his own, and invaluable to lovers of solitude counter-balanced with active lives." —**David James Duncan**, author of *The Brothers K* and *Sun House*

An
Island
to
Myself

THE PLACE OF **SOLITUDE** IN AN ACTIVE LIFE

Michael N. McGregor

MONKFISH
BOOK PUBLISHING COMPANY
RHINEBECK, NEW YORK

Paperback ISBN 9781958972748
eBook ISBN 9781958972755

Library of Congress Control Number 2025002065

Book and cover design by Colin Rolfe

Monkfish Book Publishing Company
22 East Market Street, Suite 304
Rhinebeck, New York 12572
(845) 876-4861
monkfishpublishing.com

for Sylvia

All I ask of life are times like this, times of peacefulness when I can con-template. I don't mind rushing about and dealing with difficult people. I don't mind having to work at something that doesn't mean much in order to pay for food and a place to live. I don't mind difficulties that are beyond my control or sickness or tiredness. These are life. I ask only that in the midst of them I can come to a quiet place—inside or out— where I can write and learn peace and truth.

from a journal entry written on Patmos, September 27, 1992

Contents

The First Encounter

However young,
The seeker who sets out upon the way
Shines bright over the world.

Buddha, *Dhammapada*

The old bus moves too slowly down the boulevard and then the narrow streets, the broken pavement jarring my bones as I try to calm myself. Remain patient. If I'm meant to make it, I'll make it, I think. But my adrenal glands say otherwise. You *have* to make it, they insist. You *need* to get there. I glance down at the backpack I've worn through five months of constant travel and the small typewriter I found in an Athens store yesterday. All I want is to find an island and a room and start writing. But first I have to catch the ferry—and I'm late.

To distract myself, I think of the meeting in my hotel room that made me late—of the man a friend from home had asked me to contact. When he looked at the schedule and saw the ferry's first stop, he said, "Patmos. That's a beautiful island."

"Okay," I replied. "I'll go there."

But now, as the bus lumbers on, it doesn't seem I'm going anywhere. At least today. I chose the ferry I chose because it's the last one leaving Piraeus this afternoon. If I miss it, I'll have to wait till tomorrow. There's no reason I can't wait but, as my glands suggest, I don't want to wait. It seems I've waited too long already.

When the jangling finally ends and the door opens, I rush off the bus, but I can't find a sign in English anywhere. Moving as fast as I can with a pack on my back and a portable typewriter dangling from my fingers, I race down cracked sidewalks past storefronts and doorways in cheap buildings, looking for water. Emerging at last upon the concrete apron skirting the harbor, I see ships and empty berths with wooden boards announcing destinations. But none of them is mine. As the minutes tick away, I scan board after board until I see, at the end of the quay, one last ferry. Its loading ramp lolls like a tired tongue across the concrete. *Ialyssos* is stenciled on its aging hull. "Patmos?" I ask the unshaved man beside it and he shouts, "*Neh! Neh! Neh!*" as he waves me onboard. The hold he points me to is dark and stinks of diesel fumes and caked grime. The vehicles inside are mostly geriatric trucks, the canvas covering their loads stained by soot and lashed with rope. When my eyes adjust to the lack of light, I see the cleated stairs that lead up to the passenger rooms and start to climb. Only then do I believe I've really made it. I'm headed to the islands. I'm going to *write*.

The first room I come to looks like a bar, with a low ceiling, tables fastened to the floor, and dark-haired men in shabby coats drinking from plastic cups. A second room is filled with stiff-backed chairs upholstered in vinyl and arranged in rows, like those on airplanes. As in the bar, the air is thick with cigarette smoke, but here there are women as well as men, some sitting on the floor in kerchiefs and black clothes with striped bags stuffed with goods beside them. The room looks decades old and I wonder if the boat is safe in winter seas, but I'm too hungry from skipping lunch to wonder for long. Finding the cafeteria, I buy a cheap plate of chicken and a salad and settle at a table in the sun.

Suddenly, the engines thrum to life and a joy wells up inside me. It's one day after my twenty-seventh birthday and I'm alone in a way I've never been, bound for a place I've never seen, where I know no one.

And yet we have all known flights when of a sudden, each for himself, it has seemed to us that we have crossed the border of the world of reality; when, only a couple of hours from port, we have felt ourselves more distant from it than we should feel if we were in India; when there has come a premonition of an incursion into a forbidden world whence it was going to be infinitely difficult to return.

Antoine de Saint-Exupéry, *Wind, Sand and Stars*

In the five months before I caught that ferry in January 1985, I'd traveled with a friend through most of the countries in western Europe and a few in the communist east as well. Our odyssey had culminated in a three-day bus-and-railroad journey over snowy roads and icy passes that took us the length of Yugoslavia, through northern Greece, and into Athens. Except for being hauled off a train at midnight when it was thirty below and forced to return to Berlin because our Czechoslovakian visas had expired, those last days traveling south were the hardest of the entire trip. At least for me.

Without thinking, I'd sipped tap water in Dubrovnik, the consequences of which had given new meaning to the name of the train we took from there: the Titograd Express. The six-hour ride to the dictator's city was followed by a ten-hour romp over Serbian hills on a bus so crowded and a road so narrow, I thought every curve would be our last. Somehow, as my stomach roiled and my head throbbed, the driver wove his way past horse-pulled carts and ox-drawn sleds on cliffs I couldn't see the bottom of. When we finally made it to Athens, the solid ground and warmer sun steadied my stomach, but even there we kept moving. With only two days before my friend flew home and I began my search for an island, we blitzed our way through the Acropolis, the Agora, the Plaka, and every museum we could find. By the time we hugged goodbye—on a street in central Athens on the afternoon of my birthday—I'd been moving so much for so long with so many people around, it took me a moment to realize I was alone.

Even then, where I was was filled with people and the memory of my friend, and I had things to do before I caught that bus to the harbor. In addition to buying the Olivetti and leaving my camera to be cleaned, I stopped at an English-language bookstore, where I purchased a dozen cheap books to read during my time alone; the American Express office, where I picked up mail from home and exchanged money; the post office, where I sent off my winter boots; a travel agency, where I bought a ticket for my flight back to the States months later; and the telephone office, where I called my mother. An eighteen-minute call cost as much as I would pay for half a month's lodging when I reached the islands, but it was my birthday and she was my mother and I didn't know when I'd be able to talk to her again. She was as surprised as anyone when I quit my job as an editor for a relief and development magazine to travel in Europe and try to figure out how I should live. But she trusted me and supported my desire to find my way, even when it took me to an island far from her.

In those days before smartphones and the internet, when transatlantic calls were absurdly expensive, almost all of my communication with those back home took place through letters. Because we were always on the move, my friend and I had arranged for those we cared about to write to us at pre-set locations (mostly American Express offices), which meant that news and even answers to the simplest questions took weeks to reach us. The emotions that come from being distant from loved ones were more familiar to us than they are to almost anyone today.

One of the last things I did that birthday evening, in the tiny sink in the corner of my small room, was shave off the beard I'd worn for several years. I thought of my shaving as a ritual or even a sacrament. A cleansing and freeing of myself from the past in preparation for new birth. I thought about shaving my head too, but it was the middle of winter and that seemed a bit extreme. I was heading into a time of solitude, not a monastery. And I didn't want to frighten the islanders.

Although I'd spent days alone as a child and lived alone for several years, I'd rarely been away from people for more than a few hours at a time. And I'd never sought solitude consciously. As I headed into what I considered the Great Unknown, I was excited and scared and, as my shaving suggests, prepared to let the experience change me. In fact, I wanted it to change me—to rid me of ties and concerns that held me back while opening up new pathways, both neural and vocational. I knew the change that came might not be comfortable or even welcome, but I felt sure my willingness and courage would be rewarded in some way.

My confidence was bolstered by the book I read during most of the ten-hour crossing to Patmos. I'd found it in the tiny lobby of the guesthouse I was staying in and thought I'd read it until it became too loopy for me. On the long, arduous trip through Yugoslavia, I'd slogged through a dry history of Christianity. This book promised to be a lollypop after eating my spinach. But it turned out to be much more than that. I began to feel, in fact, that my discovery of it was preordained—that it had been placed on that lobby table specifically for me to find.

The book was actress Shirley MacLaine's *Out on a Limb*, the story of her journey through a variety of New Age practices that opened her up to spiritual experiences of many kinds. The book was an instant bestseller when published in 1983, but it also made MacLaine a laughing stock in some circles. That's because the subjects she addressed included not only reincarnation and meditation but also the channeling of spirits and encounters with UFOs. Some of her thoughts were too far-out even for me, especially her talk about extraterrestrials, but in a way they were central to what I took from the book, which was the need to be open to anything. I accepted that what she presented were her true beliefs. And her willingness to search for them, examine them, and express them made me want to do the same. What better preparation could there be for an extended period of solitude?

When I finished the book, I rose from where I was sitting—in a corner out of the wind on the boat's rear deck—and walked to the railing to look at the stars. The first ones I saw were those in the cluster known as the Pleiades, which I'd discovered while working as a firefighter on the flanks of Mt. Hood during my college summers. It had seemed since then that they were *my* constellation, shining down to reassure me wherever I was. As my eyes turned toward the seamless rise and fall of the sea, it occurred to me that no one knew exactly where I was. If I were to fall in and drown, no one would know. Thinking of death might have made me feel gloomy but MacLaine's assurance that death is not the end—something I'd long accepted but never really thought about—gave me a peaceful feeling instead. It wasn't her assurance so much as the possibility that calmed me. Her book was a book about possibilities—about believing that an increase in spiritual awareness of any kind can move the self—and even the world—in a better direction.

The timid mind shuts this window with a bang, and is silent and thoughtless about what it does not know in order to chatter the more about what it thinks it knows. It fills up the uncharted spaces with mere repetition of what has already been explored. But the open mind knows

*that the most minutely explored territories have not really been known
at all, but only marked and measured a thousand times over. And the
fascinating mystery of what it is that we mark and measure must in
the end "tease us out of thought" until the mind forgets to circle and
pursue its own processes, and becomes aware that to be at this moment
is pure miracle.*

Alan Watts, *The Wisdom of Insecurity*

As our scheduled arrival at Patmos approaches, the world
beyond the ferry lights is lost in a blackness that seems a kind of
emptiness too, as if we aren't crossing the Aegean alone but the
universe itself. Undulating below us, the seas are unusually calm
for winter, like the arms of a mother rocking her child in the dead
of night. I will learn later that the seas can become so violent this
time of year it's impossible for the ferry to enter the narrow defile
that leads to the Patmos harbor, but on this night even the largest
swells are only nudging us along.

Because I've seen nothing from the deck but stars for hours,
it takes me a moment to realize the brighter lights I notice in the
lower sky are something else. They cross the blackness in strings
with nothing below them, like streetlamps lighting the parkways
of some celestial city. I don't know yet that these are the lights of
Chora, the town that surrounds the monastery on the island's
highest hill. On future visits I'll watch for them—for the way
they appear suddenly and welcomely in the dark, like a kind word
on a hard day. Coming from a country where even the rural areas
are often over-lit, I have no context for what I'm seeing: lights
that hover over a blackness almost absolute.

Marooned in the middle of the Aegean, miles from land of
any kind, Patmos in those days was blessedly free from the light
pollution that affects so much of our overbuilt world. In winter,

in particular, when the tourists were gone and the restaurants closed, the islanders felt no need to waste expensive energy on something as frivolous as gratuitous lighting. During that first visit, I'd come to appreciate this as much as anything else. When I walked at night or gazed across a sweep of land, my eyes could rest on what they saw without the glare of modern times.

Thinking about that darkness now, I can see how much trust what I was doing called for. But I didn't think in those terms then. I was doing what I was doing because I wanted to, and it seemed a benevolent presence was blessing my journey. I don't mean I felt called or even led to do it. The compulsion came from within me. But I can see now that I was trusting everyone and everything, from the Spirit I believed in, to the man who recommended Patmos, to the skill and judgment of the ferry's crew. I was trusting that the island I was bound for would offer me a place to stay and food to eat and the islanders would treat me kindly or at least indifferently. I was trusting that my health would last and world leaders wouldn't blow up the planet while I was ignorant of world news. I was trusting as well that what I was doing would enhance my life, if only because I dared to do it.

One day, years later, when I had started leading tours through Europe, including Greece, I coaxed a group of travelers across a busy street in Athens by telling them, "Just walk steadily, without sudden moves or stops, and the cars will weave their way around you." I'd discovered this in Italy and found it worked in Greece as well. The drivers there were more aware and less rigidly confined by lines and rules than their American counterparts. This gave their driving a jazz-like quality, with shifts and counter-shifts, incorporations and improvisations. They didn't realize it, of course, but their driving had a kind of harmony. There wasn't a pattern you could predict but rather a flow you could enter, like wading into a stream.

When my group reached the other side without incident, a

woman I'd known for several years turned to me and said, "Now I know the difference between you and me. You trust the world." Her words were mostly true. But mine was not a blind trust. It came from awareness turned into theory and then practice.

By the time the *Ialyssos* threads its way between the dark, constricting rocks into the open bowl of the Patmos harbor, I've done enough traveling in my life to believe that anywhere a public conveyance arrives, lodging of some kind will be available. I stay on the open deck in the winter cold to watch the stern's slow swing toward a low-lit quay and hear the clang of the chains as the loading ramp descends. From where I stand, I can see the portside buildings, a couple of roads, and the darkened white-wash of cube-like structures spilling down from a high ridge. I can't wait to wake up in the morning and explore. But first I have to find a place to sleep. My eyes scour the dark and quiet port town, Skala, and there, down a thin alley, I spy a small hexagonal sign that says: *Hotel Rex*.

Moments later, I've made my way past the disembarking trucks and the locals hugging loved ones to the hotel's door, where a somber older woman greets me. She's dressed entirely in black but has a presence that's more inviting than any smile at any American hotel. In the years ahead, this woman will welcome me again and again, always in the same calm and unsmiling manner, and I will come to think of her as the island's concierge. This time, she leads me to a spartan room on the second floor with simple furniture and a window that looks out onto the harbor. As soon as she's gone, I throw the window open and watch, like a movie on a screen, the ferry ease away. The chains clang as the ramp goes up and I can hear the crew shout to each other. As people move along the quay toward home, the boat, with its docking lights still lit, slides slowly toward a dark hill and a small chapel. Part of me wants to yell *Wait!* and rush back onboard. But I stay where I am and watch the ferry disappear as if gobbled up. In the sudden quiet in the dark room, I feel the reality of what I've done and where I am: alone on speck in a vast sea 6,000 miles from home.

Almost no one today is ever alone in the way I was then. Even if we choose solitude, we know we can access something nearby that will put us in touch with someone we know in an instant. What aloneness like that does is force you to move forward without assurances of any kind. I had met one older woman who might or might not have been as kind as I imagined. I talked in my way to a God who seemed to be somewhere nearby but was silent. I thought my body, mind, and emotions were stable. But lesser things have broken greater people. I was on my way to finding out just who I was.

For now she need not think of anybody. She could be herself, by herself. And that was what now she often felt the need of—to think; well not even to think. To be silent; to be alone. All the being and the doing, expansive, glittering, vocal, evaporated; and one shrunk, with a sense of solemnity, to being oneself, a wedge-shaped core of darkness, something invisible to others...and this self having shed its attachments was free for the strangest adventures.

Virginia Woolf, *To the Lighthouse*

The following morning, I pay for my room, leave my things at the hotel, and rush outside to see the island. Any fears I had about the downside of being alone are gone. The weather is sunny and cool, perfect for a first day in the Greek islands. I've heard of people riding motorbikes in Greece and think that might be a good way to see the whole island quickly. So when I notice a rental shop a few steps from the Rex, I go inside. As I do, I notice an advertisement for an apartment in the window. It seems the universe is on my side. The woman who greets me, however, tells me the bikes are all in the shop this time of year and I just missed the man with the apartment. She gives me his name and where he lives. Then, as I'm about to leave, she hands me a Patmos guidebook. It doesn't have a front cover but it does have a map on the back and a history of the island in English inside, along with descriptions of its towns and areas. I buy four oranges and a pack of cookies at a grocery store and start walking north, pausing from time to time to study the book. Alone, with the sun above me, I feel like Adam exploring the contours of Eden.

The book calls Patmos a "hiker's paradise" with goatherd paths that give you access to almost anywhere. It tells me the locals are "extremely gentle and hospitable" and says I shouldn't hesitate to ask for a glass of water or to buy whatever I see growing in fields, which doesn't really apply in January. I follow the paved road that circles the harbor, where a few small boats sway at their moorings: fishing boats painted in lively colors and what look like tourist boats with open hulls and awnings above. Beyond them I can see the far side of the bay: a high hill with some kind of outpost on it and several small buildings nearer the water. It doesn't take long to reach the end of town, and soon I'm walking along a blacktopped road past rocky hills and treeless vistas. The land looks biblical to me, with austere soil saturated in centuries of history. Each time a turn swallows the sea, it reappears somewhere in front of me, the view more beautiful than the one before.

I set my sights on a bay called Lefkes, which the guidebook's author, Tom Stone, says is only an hour away by foot. There's "a special kind of rough beauty to the place," he writes, "and an aura of recent desertion that should appeal to lovers of solitude." It's also on the island's west side, which means if I can find a room there, it might have a sunset view. Before I've gone very far, I see a whitewashed wall with chain-link fencing and barbed wire sprouting above it. I realize it surrounds a military base, a reminder that Patmos is only a few miles from the Turkish coast. In the not-too-distant past, Greece and Turkey almost came to blows, with Patmos on the front line. What feels like the end of the earth to me is the center of someone else's conflict.

When I reach the turnoff to Lefkes, men are working on the road, making it impossible to pass, so I continue on to Upper Kampos, a cluster of whitewashed buildings with a restaurant that doesn't strike me as anywhere special. The map shows a Lower Kampos that seems to be near the water, but I have my heart set on Lefkes. To bypass the construction, I take Stone's words about goatherd paths to heart and strike out across the land. Within a few minutes, I come to a thin dirt road that leads through several gates to houses grouped around a small church. The view to the west is excellent, and so, following Stone's advice again, I stop at one of the houses to ask if there are rooms available. When a woman answers my knock, I use my phrasebook and the little Italian I know to make my desire known. I'm envisioning sharing meals with a family, learning Greek through conversation, and spending my days in a quiet room with a view of the sea when the woman says, "No, there's nothing here. Try Kampos."

Unwilling to give up on Lefkes just yet, I return to the road and look for another way around the construction. Bushwhacking a path across a high hill, I find myself scrabbling over rocks where there's little to cling to. As I zigzag down toward the bay, I don't see anywhere I might stay until suddenly a large orange structure rises out of the hillside. With eaves and gables and even a tower with a sweeping view, it looks like something out of a Victorian novel, as shocking in that setting as seeing the Statue of Liberty. According to Stone, a Patmian merchant built it a few years ago, importing the materials, the decorations, and even the builders from Egypt to please his new Egyptian wife. His wife died, however, and the merchant left his mansion to crumble. I fantasize about living in the tower with that view before moving on. A few steps farther down the road, I come to the beach and climb a promontory on the far side, hoping to find another, maybe better bay beyond it. This requires clambering over large boulders and slippery hillsides but I figure if the goats can do it so can I. When I can finally see the next bay, I realize it would take all day to reach it. Admitting defeat, I return to Skala, resigned to staying somewhere more pedestrian.

Tired from my five-hour journey, I follow the directions the bike woman gave me to find Antonio, the man with the apartment to rent. He's maybe five years older than me, with a halo of black hair, a thin beard, and a friendly manner. The place he shows me is just outside of Skala on a hill where the road to Chora takes a sharp turn. It's a small complex but no one else is staying there. There's a clothesline outside and the inside is fully furnished: two single beds, a tiny bathroom, gas stove, refrigerator, dishes, and a one-person balcony from which I can see the crenelated walls of the monastery on its hilltop. The furnishings are cheap but it has everything I need—except, of course, a nearby beach or a sunset view. Because it's winter and this is a summer apartment, I'm able to talk Antonio down to $3 a day for the two months I'll be staying. I can't believe my good fortune.

When I've fetched my backpack and typewriter and stocked the small refrigerator with food from the grocery store, I write a letter to my girlfriend back home, make spaghetti for dinner, and then spread the dozen books I've brought along on one of the beds to choose my next read. Some are novels, some histories, some different kinds of nonfiction. As I try to decide which to read now, my eyes keep returning to a thin paperback I bought at the Athens bookstore for a dollar and a half: an unread 1950s reprint of Thomas Merton's autobiography, *The Seven Storey Mountain*.

At that point in my life, I'd heard about Merton but never read anything by this man whose thoughts on solitude would greatly influence my own in the years ahead. I'd come across a reference to *The Seven Storey Mountain* in a book I'd read earlier in my trip and then, coincidentally or maybe providentially, found that copy in that Athens store. Before I'd read more than a handful of pages, I knew its story of a spiritually-oriented young writer searching for his place in the world was perfect for me right then. I had no idea, however, how much reading that book at that moment would change my life.

Without solitude of some sort there is and can be no maturity. Unless one becomes empty and alone, he cannot give himself in love because he does not possess the deep self which is the only gift worthy of love. And this deep self, we immediately add, cannot be possessed. My deep self is not "something" which I acquire, or to which I "attain" after a long struggle. It is not mine, and cannot become mine. It is no "thing"—no object. It is "I."

The shallow "I" of individualism can be possessed, developed, cultivated, pandered to, satisfied: it is the center of all our strivings for gain and for satisfaction, whether material or spiritual. But the deep "I" of the spirit, of solitude, and of love cannot be "had," possessed, developed, perfected. It can only be, and act according to deep inner laws which are not of man's contriving, but which come from God.

Thomas Merton, "Notes for a Philosophy of Solitude"

I want to make it clear before I go any further that I didn't choose to live alone on the island of Patmos because I was seeking spiritual betterment. One big mistake people make when they decide to spend time alone is thinking they are isolating themselves to do "spiritual work"—to become a better Christian or Buddhist or Muslim, or simply a better person. As often as not, these people find the experience frustrating or even frightening. Instead of meeting their God in a burning bush or descending the mountain with new commandments, face aglow with holy light, they struggle with a deep, unsettling loneliness that triggers feelings of sadness and inadequacy. Troubling memories and crippling regret too. That's because the one thing solitude is certain to do is bring you face-to-face with yourself. And there's no guarantee you'll come away feeling "enlightened."

I don't mean there wasn't a spiritual aspect to my desire to be alone in the way I chose. I felt guided in some way to that place of aloneness, and I expected the experience to challenge me and maybe change me at some deeper level, though I didn't know exactly how. Although I hoped to sense a presence near me, I didn't expect that presence to keep me from loneliness or even foolish decisions. Not long before I went to Patmos, my work for the relief and development magazine included interviewing people in extreme poverty in developing countries. Some were plagued by diseases like leprosy or polio, some lacked access to adequate water or food, and some were trapped in the terrorism of endless war. Many had faith that was deeper and more profound than any I'd ever witnessed. If no God intervened to help them, why would I expect a God to intervene to keep me from something as comparatively trivial as loneliness?

The second-century saint Irenaeus of Lyons once wrote, "Gloria Dei vivens homo"—the glory of God is a man fully alive. That's what I went to Patmos to be: fully alive. I didn't go there to become a saint or even to "find myself." I went there to be myself. For me, that meant writing a novel. Seeing if I was cut out to be a creative writer. Seeing if this desire that had lived in me for years had something to do with finding a truer path, a greater awareness—of who I was and who I might become.

If all I wanted to do was write a novel, you might say, why couldn't I have returned to the States and simply avoided working at a regular job for a while, as other first-time novelists have done? My answer is: my life in Seattle, where I grew up, was full of people and habits and palimpsests of everything I'd ever been taught or believed or experienced or feared. In that atmosphere, every part of my life was overpopulated. Even on an island 6,000 miles from home, my head and heart were full of others, including other me's I had to get beyond. I wanted to see what it meant to be alone with a deeper self. Without distraction or obligation. The challenge for my soul was akin to the challenge others pursue for their bodies when they run marathons or enter Ironman competitions. I hoped a purer me would emerge—not a holier or stronger or even better me, but simply one that was unadorned and unencrusted, stripped of artifice and delusion.

For that to happen, I felt I needed three things: the isolation itself, the project I was there to work on, and a willingness to do whatever it took to sustain myself and my efforts while there. There was a fourth thing too: an honest pursuit of quiet in every way—the kind of quiet that allows a fragile being to emerge and the heart to hear a still small voice deep within.

I was afraid I wouldn't accomplish what I wanted to in the time I had if I didn't have guidelines to live by, so I laid down several rules for myself: 1. No alcohol. 2. Maintain a healthy diet, as much as that is possible on a Greek island in winter. 3. Try to write for eight hours a day, with a minimum of six; not just thinking or imagining but fingers moving over the typewriter. 4. Write every day except Sunday. 5. Exercise every day, even if it's only walking.

In retrospect, all of these rules were important, not only for getting work done but also for structuring my time and keeping me from the kinds of indulgence I was prone to. I'm no more ascetic by nature than I am a recluse, nor have I ever been very good at avoiding distractions when they seem more enjoyable than my work. As a result, that first week of writing in solitude was especially hard. I believed, though, that forcing myself to work consistently would develop habits of action and thought as surely as physical labor develops calluses that let tender hands keep working. It was Aristotle, I think, who said excellence is not an act but a habit.

One of the first things I discovered in living by these rules was that I could write without planning what came next. Maybe that had something to do with writing on a typewriter, which is slower than writing on a computer, allowing one's thoughts to keep pace. It might have had something to do with the cold as well. In what I soon discovered was an unheated concrete room, I kept my fingers moving at times just to keep them warm. Fortunately, my characters were quick to provide action and dialogue.

I believe now that writing without stopping prepared me for other things I experienced during those weeks of solitude. It kept me from over-thinking, teaching me I could stay entirely in the moment, moving forward with confidence that whatever I needed would be there, even in creating an imagined world. In other words, while using my mind, I could bypass my mind, or at least the part of it that second-guessed the intuitive part.

One of the greatest difficulties in entering solitude is letting yourself simply be there. Most of us live lives in which external things drive our days. If we don't have something we have to do, we turn to an external source to fill our time. I don't mean entertainment only. Even running errands or talking to a friend can be little more than distraction from being alone with ourselves. So often, when faced with an empty hour, we reach for something to fill it rather than letting ourselves simply be in the world, listening and waiting and trusting what comes.

How wonderful are islands! Islands in space, like this one I have come to, ringed about by miles of water, linked by no bridges, no cables, no telephones. An island from the world and the world's life. Islands in time, like this short vacation of mine. The past and the future are cut off; only the present remains. Existence in the present gives island living an extreme vividness and purity. One lives like a child or a saint in the immediacy of here and now.

Anne Morrow Lindbergh, *Gift from the Sea*

These are the things I've brought to Patmos: a large blue backpack, a smattering of clothes I wash by hand, a toothbrush and toothpaste and toiletries, a typewriter and typing paper, pens and paperbacks and a cheap blank book I write in daily, a Walkman and half a dozen cassettes, a Swiss army knife, a wool cap, sunglasses, suntan lotion, three squares of modeling clay, and a harmonica I play poorly. I've also brought: a quiet faith, eight years of Lutheran schooling, four years of public high school, four years at a state college, three years of writing about the poor, the stories of people living on the edge, the insecurity of growing up in a broken family, the love of a devoted mother, the goodwill of numerous friends, the desire to do something good for the world, the fear of inadequacy, the courage to do something new, the fear of failure, the strength of my body, the weakness of allergies, hopefulness, humility, and a deep passion for writing. It's the interaction of these with my new environment that will determine my experience of solitude, as well as each moment's reality.

I sleep well my first night in my new place and rise early to spend an hour taking a warm shower, drinking a cup of tea, and praying. Then the writing begins. The small kitchen is perched above the room where the beds are and I write at the kitchen table, working for two hours before eating cornflakes for breakfast and walking into town for more groceries. The woman behind the counter, Anna, is Australian and, for no reason other than where she works and her friendly manner, she'll become the only person I'll talk to at any length for the next month. She'll tell me eventually that she's married to the muscular man with the thick beard who wakes me up before dawn when he unlocks the metal doors below my apartment to take out the flats of soft drinks and beer he sells to local grocers. She'll tell me how she met him on the ferry to Patmos, swept up in the joy of being on vacation and seeing a handsome local. Then she'll tell me she hates it here, she and the other women from various countries with similar experiences. I want to ask why she doesn't just go home, but I know life is rarely that simple.

It *is* simple for me right now, however, and the simplicity in how I'm living is an important part of my solitude. Only in simplicity are we truly free of all that clutters our world. Only in simplicity does the outside noise soften enough for the self to step forth. But simplicity is only the beginning. For solitude to bear fruit, patience and fortitude must be added, as well as an ability to be still.

After my morning outing, I return to my writing for another two hours before going for another walk, this time up the road toward the monastery. At the first corner I come to, I see the sea through the waving branches of a eucalyptus tree and realize the scene, with its whitewashed houses and beach down below, is exactly like the one in the movie I saw in high school that made me want to visit Greece someday. It seems another sign I'm meant to be here, on this particular island.

Two more hours of writing in the afternoon bring the day's total to my required six. The writing has been hard. I've never written that long in a single day. Nor have I ever tried to write a novel. Needing a break and some exercise, I change clothes and jog uphill to where the whitewashed mound that covers the

Grotto of St. John juts out from the hill. It's claimed that John wrote the book of Revelation here while exiled on Patmos, living in his own extreme solitude. To my disappointment, the grotto is closed, but a priest in a black robe and a long white beard sits on the whitewashed wall outside it. We exchange a few words in simple English and then I just sit beside him, aware of how helpful it is for my solitude to be somewhere I can't speak the language. Even sitting beside someone, my soul can be quiet, my thoughts free from interruption.

That evening, I play my Walkman for a while, letting myself indulge in the feelings music sets loose, including a longing for home. Like theater for the ancient Greeks, it purges me of emotions that might lead me astray, cleansing my heart and driving me back into the story I'm writing, where deep emotions are useful. Although I've done my required writing for the day, I return to the typewriter, in part because tomorrow is Sunday, my day of rest. I find, to my great delight, that the writing that was hard in the morning has grown easier now. My fingers fly across the keys, my mind absorbed in the lives and world of my characters.

Is that the night the dreams begin? Or do they come later, after I've burrowed down through layers of living and memory rimed over my soul? I will learn in time that solitude tends to begin in euphoria, the ersatz joy of new experience, but soon—often shockingly soon—something reminds you you're alone, not just in ways you want to be but also in ways you don't. When cold seeps in and your nose runs and you shiver under five cheap blankets in a room where the walls do little more than hold the chill and moisture, you begin to understand what 6,000 miles means. What having no one to call means. Even, to some extent, what death means. But you begin to understand what kindness means as well. What family means. Connections. Your eyes weep not from allergies alone but also because the absence of things you once took for granted makes you grateful even for the socks you have to wear to bed. The tea you drink in the morning. The letters you know will come eventually from those you've told where you are.

Night, you learn, is when the most interesting and frightening things happen. When your mind, your memory, and your imagination come most fully alive. Lying there, with the day's work over, you begin to truly *feel*—not the borrowed feelings of music but feelings that can seem too real. While your mind controls your thoughts by day, something else rules the night. It whispers intimations of deeper sensations. Deeper comforts. Deeper pains. Although the world around you is silent, you know in a way you don't by day that a presence is there with you. Although you've traveled with someone for months, sleeping every night in the same room, you've never known a presence like this one—one so fully inside and out, the difference between the two doesn't matter. You don't feel you're floating on some celestial plane, yet all around seems both real and unreal at the same time, and the line between sleeping and waking grows increasingly nebulous.

If it isn't that first night the dreams begin, it's the second or third, close enough to your arrival that you think their vividness comes from giving up alcohol, restaurant food, chocolate. Depriving yourself of these things, it seems, has released some chemical. The dreams aren't all enjoyable. Some would qualify as nightmares. But there is one that comes to you one night you know you'll always remember. One that seems to explain why you're here, on this island, seeking a truer and freer life.

That's what it is, isn't it? You want to be freer. You sense that being freer to decide how you live is tantamount to living a truer life. Until now, you've lived a life in which right and wrong, good and evil, have been defined for you. The church you grew up in had its rules. Conservative rules. Rules that fit you no better as you grew than a jacket you wore in grade school. You remember the time you started a round of applause for a person who'd staged a children's show and a friend raised in the same congregation admonished you, "We don't clap in church." Why not? you asked him silently. And now, in this place you've come to after seeing suffering among the poor that made the platitudes and talk of God in safe white churches sound appallingly empty, those rules are losing their grip. Away from the scrutiny of others, you feel the freedom to decide for yourself what you believe, how you will act, what is right for you, and what is wrong. Yet, as the rules drift away, you snatch at them to pull them back. They're the armor the church convinced you you needed, and although you wonder now what you ever needed them for, it's hard to just relinquish them. What will take their place? you wonder. What beyond your own experiences and moral reactions will guide you going forward?

But then you feel that presence again. And you know that presence offers the answer. But what if it leaves me? you ask. What if it disappears when I need it most? What if someone insists my movement beyond my old church is misguided? Someone I trust. Where will I be then? How will I handle being alone? Standing alone. Knowing the people I've known all my life will think I've gone astray.

You know—in the quietest times, the deepest moments—these questions don't really matter. Once you've discovered truth, even a truth that's true only for you, you have to follow it. The truth, as Jesus said, will set you free. One of the virtues of solitude you've encountered already is that you can apprehend the truth more easily without the noise at home. The distractions and countering voices. All you need to do once you've apprehended it is trust it's true for you.

This is where the dream comes in. In it, you stand at the back of a church like the one you grew up in. The lighting is bright, like a movie set, and near the front musicians are blowing trumpets, as they do sometimes on Easter morning. The church is filled with people you know, but there in the back, behind a pillar, there are only a few, most of them young. As the trumpets play, a girl you haven't seen before begins to dance, and although you wonder if it's okay to dance while a service is going on, you begin to dance too. When the trumpets dip, the girl dips, so you do too. You worry what the congregation will think, but the girl is enjoying herself—and so are you—so you keep dancing. The feeling you feel—there in that church, there in that dream—is a feeling of pure joy. Not the joy that comes to some when they break rules but the joy that comes from being fully alive. You're wearing clothes in the dream but it wouldn't matter if you were naked. You know the biblical source for how you're feeling: you're David, God's beloved, dancing before his Lord. When you remember the dream the next morning, tears will fill your eyes because you'll know the dance you were dancing was the dance of truth. The dance of freedom. And you'll know you'll never go back to living or believing as you once did.

If this one dream, this one understanding, were all that living alone on Patmos produced, it would have been enough. But telling the story the way I have, emphasizing the feelings and freedom and sense of truth, implies that all I lived through there was only the means to an end, the exploits and sufferings of an eventually conquering hero. Here, though, is the greater truth I learned: everything—all of it—enriches you. Strengthens you. And, yes, enlightens you. Even if there were no joy, no dreams, no understanding, the experience would be worthwhile because it brings you face-to-face with a stripped-down reality. It's as valuable to learn you can be broken down by cold and molds and dust as it is to discover you can live without the sound of a single human voice or enter a realm where the borders between night and day, sleeping and waking, dreaming and memory disappear. We are everything we are—body, mind, spirit, emotion, hormone, bacteria, DNA—and it is in suffering as much as wellness that we discover the fullness of what that means.

When you have closed your doors, and darkened your room, remember never to say that you are alone, for you are not alone; God is within, and your genius is within——and what need have they of light to see what you are doing?

Epictetus, *Discourses*

Night is when solitude cracks us open. It's at night I feel so cold, fully clothed, with five blankets over me, I finally go to Antonio and ask him for a heater. Some misguided part of me has equated aloneness with endurance. It has made me think solitude means doing everything on my own, even if that leads to destruction. Nothing could be more mistaken. The pride that such a stance exposes is part of what solitude is meant to dismantle. It's not in suffering from cold or allergies I learn; it's in my response to them, the need for help they lead me to. When Antonio hands me the small aluminum dish with the heating coils inside and I set it up beside my bed, careful to keep the polyester blankets away, the warmth I feel—the warmth that lets me close my eyes and sleep deeply—comes as much from having allowed another person to help me as from the physical relief the heater provides.

Night is when I doubt myself. Night is when the people I've hurt visit me and ask why. Night is when I wonder if I should have lived differently. Night is when my mind fills with questions without answers, some personal, some abstract, some about whether there is any meaning to be found in a human life at all. Night is when I'm aware of the void of space, the distances between stars, the unfathomable question of where life or anything comes from. Night is when my beliefs face challenge and when there is no belief at all, just existence in a dark space, a passing moment, the room behind my eyes where everything seems illusory.

But night is also where the line between remembering and imagining blurs, where thoughts bleed into dreams so I don't know in the morning which was which. Night is where, when I can't sleep, I remember my grandparents' house, where my family went on holidays and Sundays until I was ten and my grandfather died. To my astonishment, I remember everything, not in some vague way but in precise detail.

Lying there in the dark with nothing to distract me, nothing to disturb my concentration or remind me that I'm somewhere else, I find I can go anywhere in the house—through any door into any room—and picture what was there. I can see the black wallpaper with its colorful flecks in the single bathroom, the porcelain sink with its mirror and light, and the tub where I'd lie alone as long as I could, warm and secure. I can see the pictures hung in the bedroom behind doors and the dresser and vanity my grandmother gave me years later. I can smell the rusty screen over the attic window I slept beside on summer nights and picture the half-wall hiding the winter clothes, the light I read my Seuss books by. I can see the kitchen's swinging door with its ivory paint, the oven my grandmother baked her cookies in, and the alcove where my grandfather ate his Uncle Sam cereal, tipping his bowl away from him to scoop out the last of it. I can hear the voice on the plastic radio give the daily bingo numbers we checked against the playing pieces we brought from the grocery store.

How amazing it is to find it all there in my mind: the open stairs to the basement, the second refrigerator with its five-gallon tub of vanilla ice cream, my grandfather's work bench with his tools above, and the room in the back filled with extra furniture. Even the yard and garden are vivid in my mind: the smell and brush of the evergreens beside the front porch when we crouched there for Hide 'n Seek, the raspberries we picked off the metal wires my grandmother trained them onto, and the red and pink roses that grew nearby, their scent sweeter still than any rose I've smelled since.

How many things still lie in our memory, capable of being recalled in such detail? How many smells and sounds, sights and tastes, joys and pains that can bring the past so close it feels present? In truth, we are never alone. The more alone we become, the more porous our minds become as well. We think we've shut out the world, but removing the present we've been moving through only calls forth the past we've kept distant. My memories of my grandparents' place are sweet and grow sweeter in detail, but solitude opens the door to other memories as well: places and people that frightened us, times we struggled with sadness, moments like those I spent as a child in the bottom of a cardboard refrigerator box, its open end tipped toward the sky. It was there, in that box, I felt safe on my own for the first time, happy to be alone in a place no one could find me. Is there a line from then to now, I wonder, a pleasure in solitude that comes from having been still in the midst of an insecure childhood? Could such a thing exist already in a small boy?

The questions and images that come at night, unbidden but not unwelcome, aren't always linear in appearance. Nor do they always coalesce or lead to anything in particular. They rise, it seems, through the vitreous of my being, as if caught somewhere far below and freed by my lack of distraction to rise into consciousness. When I let go of my need to find a pattern in them or even react to them, they show me, one by one, what amazing organisms I and my fellow humans are. As we go about our busy lives, we live in ignorance of our many dimensions, abilities, and possibilities. It is only in solitude that they become free to manifest themselves—to show that no matter what the world around us says, we are more capable, numinous, and profound than we've ever been led—or allowed—to believe.

Our deepest fear is not that we are inadequate. Our deepest fear is that we are powerful beyond measure. It is our light, not our darkness, that most frightens us. We ask ourselves, who am I to be brilliant, gorgeous, talented, fabulous? Actually, who are you not to be? You are a child of God. Your playing small doesn't serve the world. There's nothing enlightened about shrinking so that other people won't feel insecure around you. We are all meant to shine, as children do. We were born to make manifest the glory of God that is within us. It's not just in some of us; it's in everyone. And as we let our own light shine, we unconsciously give other people permission to do the same. As we're liberated from our own fear, our presence automatically liberates others.

Marianne Williamson, *A Return to Love*

Sitting and writing in a quiet room is one kind of solitude, a kind where structure and focus serve me well, calling me back to a purpose whenever my mind strays. Lying alone at night is a different kind, one that allows my mind and spirit to range through memory, emotion, and imagination. But there are other kinds too, each beneficial in its own way. That first Sunday, for example, I feel free to do nothing at all except wander without purpose or destination. Because I'm alone, beholden to no one, even myself—my own plans or hopes or expectations—I'm awake to the world, to random encounters, to beauty that comes from places I wouldn't expect it. Freed from the pledge to work that governs every other day, I intend to sleep in before anything else. But a violent storm awakens me and I rush out to rescue the clothes I washed and hung out to dry before bed. By the time

I have my clothes inside, they—and I—are thoroughly soaked. But here's where the random beauty comes in. It's the soaking that makes me aware of the warmth in my bed as I slip back in, the rain that makes me appreciate the sun that is out when I wake up again, and the thunder that makes the birds' soft tweets sound so delicate and peaceful.

After a time of silent prayer and reading about Merton's life, I take a hot shower and put on clean clothes for the first time in several days, thankful, after the storm, for the water's warmth and the clothes' freshness. When I exit the house, I leave my watch behind and climb the hill toward the monastery, slowly and mindfully. The sound of the storm, the cold of the rain, the warmth of the bed, the shine of the sun, the song of the birds, the calm of the prayer, the words of the book, the heat of the shower, and the touch of the clothes have opened my senses to everything. My solitude today, I see, will be a physical kind, a sensuous kind, a kind that welcomes the world rather than shutting it out.

The road curves back on itself several times and the view looks lovelier at every corner. One turn gives a glimpse to the east, where islands rise in the endless sea. The next one gives a look to the west, where nothing appears to mar the surface. From everywhere, at every step, the land to the north is visible, with bright-white cubes on low-slung hills reflecting the morning sun. The higher I climb, the whiter the buildings appear against the sapphire blue of the sea.

Just before I reach the monastery, I pass two men with a team of donkeys. The men are old but the hill doesn't faze them. They greet me with smiles and happy shouts as if to celebrate my own ascension. And the view I have from the top is worth celebrating. For the first time since arriving I can see the whole island, including the lusher lands to the south, where the road passes through green fields. Before descending that direction, I round the monastery's ramparts and slip into its sheltered courtyard. There's no one inside but the gatekeeper, who leaves me alone as I gaze at the frescoes, worn and scarred and full of religious scenes.

I see a date—1738—carved into a doorframe and check my guidebook to see what happened then. It doesn't mention that year, but it tells me the monastery, with its high stone walls, was begun in the eleventh century under the guidance of a monk named Ioannis Christodoulos. Christodoulos, the book says, found the island "covered with brambles and thorny scrub, untrodden and so arid as to be totally barren and infertile." After securing the right to possess it from Byzantine ruler Alexius I Comnenus, he turned it into a place of prayer akin to Mount Athos. Lying where it did, however, it couldn't escape the incursions of marauding groups: Normans, Arabs, Turks, Crusaders, and a regular succession of pirates seeking the riches rumored to be behind the monastery's walls. So the monks of old had their distractions too.

Despite its history, Patmos has been a symbol of solitude through the ages, mostly because of its link to St. John—his exile and his visions. French author Victor Hugo, who exiled himself to the Channel Islands, saw Patmos as a metaphor for being enlarged by the kinds of visions and meditations a chosen solitude makes possible. "Every man has within him his Patmos," Hugo wrote. "He is free to go, or not to go, out upon that frightful promontory of thought from which one perceives the shadow. If he does not, he remains in the common life, with the common conscience, with the common virtue, with the common faith, or with a common doubt; and it is well. For inward peace, it is evidently the best. If he goes out upon those heights, he is taken captive. The profound waves of the marvelous have appeared to him. No one views with impunity that ocean. Henceforth he will be the thinker, dilated, enlarged, but floating; that is to say, the dreamer. He will partake of the poet and of the prophet." This is solitude writ large—the power it has to change our vision, our understanding, and ultimately our lives.

It was during his voluntary seclusion on Guernsey that Hugo did his most original writing and finished his masterpiece, *Les Misérables*, whose scenes of passion and sympathy for the poor continue to touch readers and theatergoers. Hugo's view of what is possible when you dare to be alone with yourself might seem too grand, but it is justified by his life and work. It's also consistent with the power I felt myself in touch with during my time alone on the actual Patmos. I sensed that even a glimpse of the ocean within me from the promontory of solitude had the power to change my relationship to the life I'd lived and to life in general.

Standing here in this courtyard with these thick walls around me, I think of the monks who live and have lived within them, whose dedication to solitude, like that of Merton, far outstrips my own. For them, solitude is a path that leads ever deeper inside without a turning back or turning away from the "profound waves of the marvelous." In the Merton book I'm reading, he mentions a sign he noticed over a doorway in the monastery he entered at about the same age I am as I read about him. *God Alone*, it said. For a monk, God is found most readily and completely in aloneness. But for me, solitude is only one of many avenues to God. Choosing to be alone is like focusing on the vivid red in a rainbow. I have no doubt the red a monk like Merton sees is more profound and sublime than the one I do. But I find the rainbow's green numinous too. And its indigo. And its violet. Alluring as red can be for a time, my soul craves the full spectrum.

Before I continue my journey south, I wander the narrow streets of Chora, whose lights I saw on the ferry before I saw the land. Voices spill through open doorways in the long white walls, making it seem as if everyone is enjoying a social Sunday afternoon, but I see no one until I'm back on the main street and pass a boy and girl arm-in-arm. For the first time, then, my commitment to this solitude wavers. I think of my girlfriend back home and feel a longing for someone to share this beauty with. Before the feeling has passed, I come across an old woman with a black shawl draped across her crippled back. She's walking with the same companions I saw her with yesterday: two boys and two goats. Then, she was trying to stop the boys from pulling the rope attached to one goat's neck. Now, she has each boy by the hand and seems to be telling them something for their own good. She's smiling, as she was yesterday, and her relationship with the boys reminds me of mine with my own grandmother. Again I feel a longing, this time for the comfort of having stable, caring family nearby.

Until now, I've thought of solitude as living quietly, separated from others, but this day is teaching me that solitude is mostly just a state of being. It doesn't exclude people or the world around us but simply keeps one's thoughts and energies to oneself instead of expending them in interaction. There can be movement in solitude and solitude in movement. In fact, if not overdone, moving through the world can enhance solitude as much as reading or working on a project, providing stimulus for thought and self-reflection. The one important thing is to avoid being drawn into conversation or activity that interrupts the stillness inside. The same is true for memories: they can be valuable fodder for contemplation but they can also be disruptive, causing us to argue in our minds with people who aren't present or regret actions we can neither change nor find our way beyond. It is difficult in solitude to be both open to the world and protective, accepting what comes to us from outside or inside without engaging with it or losing our footing.

When I think of movement in relationship to solitude, I think of the words attributed to the Korean sage Do Hyun Choe: *Stillness creates love. Movement creates life. To be still and still moving, this is everything.*

As I continue my meander south, I see bays and beaches far below, and then the island narrows to a few meters. Shortly after it broadens again, I come to what looks to be an abandoned quarry, where old trucks rust beside mounds of gravel. Just beyond them, in a rocky field, I spy a goatherd separating his flocks. He sends one group over the land toward me and herds the other group into a small corral made of scavenged stone. As I move downhill toward him, a dog darts toward me, his bark both furious and frightening. Before I can react, the goatherd quiets him with a single word and then greets me with another, one I know is kind though I don't know his language.

When a second dog ambles up and puts its head against my leg to be petted, I think of the different ways dogs—and people—respond to intrusions into their worlds and how much more conducive some are than others to living a peaceful life. Although the goatherd and I can't speak to each other, we stand near each other for a while, both of us smiling, and I feel grateful for the lack of a common verbal language, for the gift of resting in the presence of a gentle, simple man without the disruption of conversation. I'm reminded of the poet Rilke's words: "Love consists of this: two solitudes that meet, protect and greet each other."

A human being is a spatially and temporally limited piece of the whole, what we call the "Universe." He experiences himself and his feelings as separate from the rest, an optical illusion of his consciousness. The quest for liberation from this illusion is the only object of true religion. Not nurturing the illusion but only overcoming it gives us the attainable measure of inner peace.

Albert Einstein, in a letter to Rabbi Robert S. Marcus

The next morning, the weather has changed again, with wind and rain sweeping in. As I settle into my writing, I remember the wooden gate I passed through after my encounter with the goatherd and the pool of light the sunrays cast upon the water. As I gazed across the jagged hills tumbling toward the sea, I gave thanks for a beauty so different from what I had known and the quiet in my soul that allowed me to savor it. On the long climb back up to Chora, at the point where the island narrows, I passed three nuns in black habits and then their convent, rising up from the orange rock. In our solitudes, we passed without speaking, yet I was aware of them on their journey and surely they were aware of me on mine. As I continued up the hill alone, the sun began to set, and when I reached the top I felt both tired and melancholy. How much better for those nuns to have each other, I thought, even if they don't speak.

I have always disliked the dusk after a happy day, the feeling that joy is fading with the light, the colors disappearing from the world. Instead of lingering to watch the sun pass out of sight, I started down toward my apartment. I could feel the walking I had done in every step and wanted only to be home. But then I heard a motorbike behind me, and as I stepped aside to let it pass, the young man riding it stopped next to me. Would I like a lift, he asked in broken English, and soon I was riding silently behind him as he eased his bike around the curves, his presence and his quiet kindness driving the melancholy away.

For six straight days that week, I write all day, stopping only for lunch and sometimes a short run. It's almost as cold inside as out, with a constant wind rattling the windows. The sun appears so rarely and briefly, I hardly notice. The novel's world is where I live until each day's work is over. Sometimes it's hard for me to sit for all those hours. I want to move, to wander, to think of other things. Other times, I'm so lost in my story I can't shake it even when the writing's done. When I walk after dinner, the characters still live in my head, and when my mind finally returns to the atmosphere around me, I'm amazed to find myself in a foreign land.

Nighttime walks have become a regular part of my days. Walking through the dark is when I feel most alone. And when the doubts descend. On days when the writing has been difficult, I think of home and wonder why I'm here; wonder if any of the pages piling up are any good. You did not come here to judge, I tell myself. Only to write. All that matters is that you write as well as you can—for God, for your future, and for those at home who pray for you and believe in you. Thinking of those at home, I'm reminded of the words of St. Paul: *Therefore, since we are surrounded by so great a cloud of witnesses, let us rid ourselves of every burden and sin that clings to us and persevere in running the race that lies before us.*

Living where I live, there are three good routes for walking. I can climb the main road or the old road toward the monastery. I can descend a little-used lane that runs through the heart of Skala. Or I can follow the main road downhill, curving around my building and passing beneath a line of eucalyptus trees toward the harbor. It's this last route I choose most often. It takes me past a hotel where local men gather at night, drinking in the yellow light and watching Chinese action films. At times, when the cold and lack of company feel especially hard, I think about going in and having a beer with them, just to be around people. But I resist the temptation and keep walking, content to know they're close by.

Night after night, when I have passed the outdoor basketball court and the grove of dormant fruit trees, a small brown-and-white dog bounds out of the dark toward me. Young and full of energy, he wags his tail and lifts his nose for a pat before falling into step beside me. From time to time, he races out in front of me to flush a cat from a garbage bin, then prances back with his head held high for me to tell him, "Good boy." I don't know at first whose dog he is or where exactly he comes from, but it comforts me to have him with me. He stays beside me for as long as I walk, whether I wander past the waterfront in Skala or out the seaside road that leads eventually to Grikou.

Grikou is home to a large rock riddled with caves that show evidence of human habitation. No one knows who lived there or when, but my guidebook speculates that monks enlarged the caves between the fourth and seventh centuries when monasticism spread out from Egypt. The rock is an enticing destination, but Grikou is too far to go at night, so I usually stop at a small rocky beach not far from the outskirts of Skala. The wind is softer there and the beach is always empty. If the moon is out, the waves twinkle with a light that makes me think of pixies dancing. Even when the moon is absent, I feel less alone by the sea, with only water between me and those I love.

It's here where I let the loneliness overtake me without trying to drive it away. I've read elaborate explanations of the difference between loneliness and solitude, but in my experience each contains a portion of the other. And that is good. Solitude without a trace of loneliness might quickly become solipsistic. It's loneliness that reminds us we are connected to others. That we need their love and they need ours. On the other hand, loneliness without a sense of solitude can eat your heart away, fooling you into thinking you're not only unloved but unlovable. To retain a sense of solitude in the midst of loneliness, you must have a sense of yourself and of meaning. Of something more than what society tells you is important.

The dog never joins me on the beach, but when I climb back up to the road, he's always there to accompany me to where he first appeared. I'll learn eventually that his name is Buby and he belongs to Antonio. To me, though, he is an angel sent to blunt my loneliness and keep me from fear. In time, two other dogs will take on the same role, one of them appearing every time I walk, no matter which direction I go. Each has the same buoyant spirit Buby does and each drops away a few meters before I reach home. If angels exist, I think, why can't they come as dogs, gentle companions on a dark road?

It's on one of these walks, when I have written enough to know that I will definitely complete a full draft of my first novel, that I begin to see myself differently than I did before. Long before traveling to Patmos—even before I studied journalism at the University of Oregon or took that first job writing about the poor—I envisioned myself as a creative writer. But I feared I wasn't good enough to do this thing I wanted to do. Moving to Patmos, in fact, was my attempt to live that vision out—to see if Thoreau was right when he said if you move confidently in the direction of your dreams you will meet with a success unexpected in common hours. It was, in effect, the crossing of my own Rubicon: an action from which there'd be no turning back.

On this particular night, the moon is full and the wind and clouds are gone. As I turn toward the beach where the pixies dance, Buby loping at my side, a Dan Fogelberg song plays in my head. The lyrics speak of moonlit nights keeping the singer from feeling alone. They end with a vision of two roads diverging in the woods. One leads to "simple acceptance of life" while the other offers "sweet peace." When the singer chooses between them, his choice becomes his "release." It seems suddenly that the song is about me: how my decision to act on my vision has led to my own release—from doubt, from fear, from worry I'm not "good enough" to be a writer. I feel in that moment that I've been put on this earth to write, and I know that wherever I go, whatever I do, I always will.

If one advances confidently in the direction of his dreams, and endeavors to live the life which he has imagined, he will meet with a success

unexpected in common hours. He will put some things behind, will
pass an invisible boundary; new, universal, and more liberal laws will
begin to establish themselves around and within him; or the old laws be
expanded, and interpreted in his favor in a more liberal sense, and he
will live with the license of a higher order of beings.

Henry David Thoreau, *Walden*

Each night, when I return from walking, I try to write about
my day unless I'm too tired. Even on those nights when I have
energy, I find it more difficult to capture what has happened on a
day of solitude than a day of travel. When I was on the road, the
journey was mostly external. It's all internal now: more complex
and harder to sort out. How do you describe the movements of
the spirit, the vagaries of the emotions, the rise and fall of the
creative urge? How do you express the daily mix of joy and fear,
asperity and wonder as you try to find or forge a truer self within
the nebula of God? At times, I simply set my pen aside and try to
express my feelings in some other way.

Taking up a square of clay, I form the image of a character from
my novel, a man named Clyde who lives on the streets. I've never
made a sculpture before, but out of patience and compassion I
fashion a figure sitting on a curb with a small dog that somehow
embodies what Clyde means to me and my story. Another time,
feeling a mix of joy and melancholy, I put my harmonica to my
lips. I've never learned to play it properly, but alone in the cold on
an island where no one knows me that doesn't seem to matter.
Nor does it matter that I know only a couple of tunes. It's the
blowing out and breathing in that matters, the physical expression of emotions. Intimations. Life.

How sad, I think, that we are made to believe we can't
play an instrument or sculpt a figure just because we do it less

expertly—or merely differently. These judgments live in us like tapeworms, robbing us of strength and energy, but in solitude they fall away if we look at them objectively and defy them. Every time I pick up clay or my harmonica or even my pen I strike a blow for freedom. Not my freedom alone but the freedom of everyone to do what they want to do, express things the way they want to express them. Each time I'm alone and I disobey the voices in my head, I make it more likely I'll do the same in the company of others and encourage them to do it themselves.

I'm learning again and again in my time alone that solitude is never for yourself only. It is always also for others. By taking the time to learn about myself, quiet the voices inside and out, and elevate awareness of what's more truly in me and around me, I unleash energy and understanding that will emanate from my words and actions wherever I go.

One way I'm sharing my experiences, thoughts, and feelings already is through letters. At times, if I have the energy, I work on a single letter for an hour or more. The commitment of time is a way of honoring friends who have continued to correspond with me after months away. They are a dwindling tribe, but I don't mind. Among the benefits of my travel has been a whittling down of the many connections I had at home, a discovery of who is most willing to go to a deeper level in our relationship.

I'm well aware it's easier to divulge thoughts and even emotions in letters written while sitting by myself than when I'm with an actual person. I know that when I go home the intimacies shared with a friend when we were thousands of miles apart will be slower to surface. We might, in fact, feel embarrassed at being known too well. But one of the greatest joys of my solitude is to read and write intimate letters. In solitude, I have the time and quiet to read slowly and carefully. To ponder a friend's situation or revelation and respond appropriately. To examine and express my own private thoughts and doubts and discoveries. Because

I'm alone and it takes weeks for a response to arrive, I don't worry about another's reaction to what I write. And I find that the more I trust others—the more I reveal of what has come to me in my time alone—the more others trust me. I learn of one person's lifelong struggles with her mother, another's doubts about his marriage, a third one's worry that he won't find his place in life. In my solitude, I hold these confessions close to my heart, feeling the weight and fragility of each, and I take them one by one to God in prayer, not in hopes of a miracle or even healing but as a kind of friend of the court appealing for grace and mercy.

Then what am I—the body substance which I can see with my eyes and feel with my hands? Or am I this realization, this greater understanding which dwells within it, yet expands through the universe outside; a part of all existence, powerless but without need for power; immersed in solitude, yet in contact with all creation?

Charles A. Lindbergh, *The Spirit of St. Louis*

The day after my epiphany on the road to the beach, the sun is out and it's a Sunday, so I decide to walk all the way to Grikou. The road follows the shoreline most of the way, and with the sun glistening off the sea I feel sure that Patmos is the prettiest place in the world. It takes me forty minutes to reach the sweep of sand that curls away from the whitewashed buildings in Grikou proper. The water is still too cold for swimming, but I vow that before I leave the island I will go in at least once.

Following the curve of the bay, I come to the huge rock with its caves that sits at the end of a long isthmus. Seeing the steps the monks carved into the stone, I climb to the top where I find what looks like a catchment tank for rainwater. Then I work my way around the circumference until I come to a cave facing the sea. A heron flies out in front of me, squawking at having its perch invaded. Peering inside, I see only chalky walls and the droppings of goats. The space is as big and as round as a Volkswagen Beetle and I envision the goatherd I met the other day taking refuge here from the rain. Carefully avoiding the goat droppings, I sit and look out toward a smaller island with an upslope of green and a single building. There's an even smaller island in the distance. Other than that, all I see is sea. Out of the wind, with only this opening to look through, it feels as if I'm the only person in the world. It feels, in fact, much like it did when I sat in that refrigerator box as a child. The color of the sea ranges from a deep majestic blue to the aquamarine you see in travel posters. Knowing no one will be disturbed by my playing, I take out my harmonica and play my favorite thing to play on it, the Scottish tune "Loch Lomond," over and over. I never get it entirely right but it doesn't matter. Sitting with nothing but rock around me and little but sunlit sea in front, I am an island to myself and I feel happy.

Later that day, I find a beach on the western side with no one on it and watch the sun go down as waves play gently and musically with the beach's stones. I record the happy sounds for a birthday tape to send to my mother and, when the last of the sun disappears, climb the hill to Chora. From the top, while the daylight on the countryside is still bright, I watch the moon spread its glow over the tranquil sea, feeling none of the melancholy I felt my last time here. What I feel instead is the quiet joy I've felt since morning. This is the best of being alone, I think, this kind of slow meditation and movement through a sun-filled day.

But sunshine and happy feelings rarely last, at least on an island in winter. The following morning the clouds are back and the apartment is cold. It's all I can do to keep my fingers moving over the keys. During a break from my work, I finish reading the Merton book and, in the evening, when my writing is done, I don't feel like starting another. So I light a candle to lift my spirits and write a long letter to a troubled friend. Then I crawl beneath my five blankets.

If I'd known when I rented the apartment that it was a summer place made entirely of concrete—a place not built to hold heat—I'm sure I would have searched for somewhere else. Although I planned to live simply in my solitude, I didn't intend to deprive myself of basic needs. The more I live in this environment, however, the more I see that living at this basic level is one more way I can be alone for others. The cold reminds me of the people I met while interviewing and writing about the poor: their mud-and-wattle huts, their shanties made of cast-off wood and strips of tin, their prison cells, their bamboo shacks. I think about their failed crops and lack of food, how limited their options were when hardships of war or famine or illness reached their door. I felt guilty when I left them behind to travel, even though it was in pursuit of knowledge about the world that had forced them to live the way they lived and the answer to the question of how I should live. That guilt has faded after only six months away, the sympathy that came from being there with them in their world. The cold puts me back in touch with them in one small way. It isn't the cold per se, but living with discomfort borne of natural conditions.

When I moved into the apartment, I stocked the refrigerator and filled the cupboards. After a couple of weeks, however, I began to let the food run out, initiating a period of what I called eat-until-there's-nothing-left. Instead of going to the grocery store to find whatever I feel hungry for, I'm making my meals from whatever's left, in order to see what it's like when you can't select your diet. For three nights in a row, for example, I eat rice. I'm hungry most of the time but I feel more thankful than before for the blessings of variety, abundance, and nutrition that come to me so easily most of the time.

As with choosing solitude, choosing deprivation, however

small, can make you thankful for all kinds of things you never thought to be thankful for before. At night, when I turn the heater on, I'm grateful for the warmth despite its limits. In the morning, when I take a shower, I'm thankful for the water, hot or cold. As those who are most grateful know, gratitude begets gratitude. Soon, I'm feeling thankful for the blessing of being able to choose what I do each day, being able to read and to write, having books and paper and a typewriter, and being free to stay on an island in Greece or leave it on a whim.

As the years pass, I am coming more and more to understand that it is the common, everyday blessings of our common everyday lives for which we should be particularly grateful. They are the things that fill our lives with comfort and our hearts with gladness—just the pure air to breathe and the strength to breathe it; just warmth and shelter and home folks; just plain food that gives us strength; the bright sunshine on a cold day; and a cool breeze when the day is warm.

Laura Ingalls Wilder, *Writings to Young Women from Laura Ingalls Wilder: On Wisdom and Virtues*

Because I don't know Greek, or have a radio or television, and there are no English-language publications on the island, I live free of the interruptions that come from reading the news each day. I learn somehow what I need to know—that the temperature on the island has dropped to close to freezing—but I don't learn what's happening in world affairs or politics. I don't know where a volcano has erupted or a war broken out or some politician out-shouted another. The freedom from this knowledge and the reaction it generates helps me to focus on the writing and reading I've chosen to do. Of course I don't watch movies or TV shows either, and the internet hasn't been invented. Relief from all these stimuli and countless others that are part of my life at home calms my mind and soul and even my nervous system. It removes the layers I would normally have to cut through to reach a place of inner quiet.

It is only after I've been alone for several weeks that I realize my patience and focus have improved—not only when I'm writing or reading a book but also when I'm just sitting. Patience and focus, in turn, have improved my awareness. One day, for example, while sitting by a window looking at the fields, I see a crow flying toward me and for the first time notice how a crow flies—the way its wings rise and fall in a slow, easy pattern that reminds me of the bats we made for Halloween in fourth grade. They were attached to the ceiling by a line of thread and the slightest movement of air made their wings flap gracefully. Watching the crow, it seems as if time itself has slowed down, making it easier to see how nature looks and works.

Slowing down might be the greatest benefit of solitude. At home, everyone, including me, moves at least a half-step too fast. Having nowhere to be and no one to disappoint, I find myself moving at a pace that feels more natural—a pace that fosters revelations and fortuitous coincidences because the rhythm of my day is more in sync with the rhythms of the natural world.

Solitude and slowing down allow me to be more aware of both my emotional and visceral responses to what I'm reading. For example, many parts of Thomas Merton's autobiography elicit excitement because I identify with him as a spiritually-oriented and meaning-seeking young writer. But it is another character in his story, a friend named Robert Lax, who appeals to me on a deeper level. Lax, who comes from a Jewish rather than Christian background, seems to have all of the book's best lines, including telling Merton, when he's trying to discern his future, that he should want to be a saint. The idea strikes me as oddly as it does Merton, but Lax's follow-up makes sense: "Don't you believe that God will make you what He created you to be, if you will consent to let Him do it? All you have to do is desire it."

The idea that all you have to do is desire what you were created to be and let God turn you into it applies as much to being a writer, I think, as to being a saint. It seems confirmation of what I felt on that moonlit walk. I make a mental note to look for Lax in later Merton books when I return home, not knowing he will cross my path again much sooner than that.

There's a tradition in Christian monastic circles called *lectio divina* that goes back to the earliest monks. *Lectio divina* is Latin for "divine reading" and originally referred to the meditative reading of passages from the Bible. In his sixth-century "Rule"—precepts for right living, a "rule of life" per se, which came to govern Western monasticism—St. Benedict called for both private and communal readings by monks, to be followed by contemplation and prayer. In many monasteries and other Christian institutions today, other writings are often substituted for scripture as a way of approaching spirituality from different angles, but the three other original elements of lectio divina remain intact: meditation, contemplation, and prayer.

I haven't yet heard of this practice when I move to Patmos, but it reflects the way I approach the reading I do on the island, not only with a clearly spiritual book like Merton's, but with everything I read.

I chose the books I brought because they interested me, not because I thought they would "improve" me in some way, but I find that all of them are challenging me, exposing me to new views. New questions. Occasionally new answers. When something strikes me in one, I have the time and quiet not only to contemplate it, but to meditate on it for several minutes or several days, and sometimes that mediation leads to surprising discoveries.

For example, the book I read right after Merton's is Catherine Marshall's *Beyond Ourselves*, which features a kind of Christian inspirational writing I tend to avoid or, at most, skim. That's primarily because, as a child, I attended a Lutheran grade school five days a week, went to confirmation classes on Saturdays, and was expected to show up for church and Sunday school on Sundays. I've had my fill of the good Christian teaching these types of books usually offer. But in her discussion of God's forgiveness, Marshall puts forth the idea that we might have a deep-seated feeling of guilt in us that God has never taken away. Although I can't think of one, I have all of the symptoms she lists. So one night I kneel beside my bed and pray for release. No great guilt comes to mind but I find myself breaking down in tears, which tells me there are things inside me I can't see and might never know. This awareness alone opens new avenues in my self-perception, allowing me to accept that there is mystery inside myself.

It's that same night, when I can't sleep, that I walk through the rooms in my grandparents' house, remembering everything. I've been on the island for three weeks and this kind of thing has become a regular occurrence. As I lie in bed each night, memories come from every corner of my life and I see the faces of friends I haven't thought about in years. When I fall asleep, I dream and dream. Throughout my life I've been reluctant to end each day, but this new combination of memories and dreams makes me look forward to going to bed. It's like entering a movie theater where you don't know what kind of movie will be playing—action, adventure, romance, comedy, farce—but you know it will astonish you in some way.

Every reader finds himself. The writer's work is merely a kind of optical instrument that makes it possible for the reader to discern what, without this book, he would perhaps never have seen in himself.

Marcel Proust, *In Search of Lost Time*

For most of us, there is a limit to the benefits of unrelieved solitude, and I reach mine almost exactly a month after moving to Patmos, on the day I finish a full draft of my novel. It isn't just the completion of the project I've come to the island to work on, though. The temperature has continued to drop and the cold is making my allergies act up. The constant wind is tiring me when I walk. And spending days and nights alone has awakened a deep desire to be with other people (which, I'm beginning to see, is one of the happy results of extended time in solitude). For a month, I've contented myself with the conversations I can have with the authors of books, the friends I write letters to, the dogs who walk with me, and God—all of which can feel one-sided. Now, I long for face-to-face contact with other people, for conversations in which the response is immediate, personal, and unpredictable. So I've decided to spend a couple weeks on the mainland and return to Patmos for more solitude afterwards.

My initial response to finishing my writing is a mix of elation, melancholy, and wonder about what comes next. Isolating myself has allowed me to finish a full draft of a novel in a surprisingly short amount of time, but the speed means less than the fact that I've done it—that I dared to step away from concerns about earning a living to do the creative work I've long wanted to do. Now that I no longer have a goal in front of me, however, I feel my aloneness—and the cold—more acutely.

The night I choose to start my trip, I say a quiet goodbye to my little apartment and walk down to the port around 10 p.m. The man in the harbor police office tells me the boat will arrive at 10:30, so I settle into a doorway to wait. It seems this night is the coldest yet, with the wind off the water lowering the temperature even more. An hour passes and then two. Every part of me has grown cold and there are no lights near where I stand so I can't distract myself by reading. I'm ready to go back and sit by my little heater when a voice inside me says, *Use this time to focus on God.*

I've never heard a voice like this before and I do my best to obey it—to give thanks for the cold and the wait and how they are teaching me to be trusting—but my mind keeps shifting back to my shivering body. Then the voice speaks again. *If you will endure,* it says, *God will bless you, and the blessing will be all the better because of the privations you have withstood.* Despite the stilted diction, I believe this voice to be divine and I stay where I am.

Within minutes, a man about my age in a beard and simple clothes approaches. In accented English, he asks if I know when the ferry will come. My *no* is the only other word we exchange, but he stays there beside me, and when we finally see the lights of the ferry appear, we board it together. Then another man, an older man, falls into step beside me and introduces himself as Jeff from Australia. After a month of talking to no one but Anna, I end up sitting between these two on the boat's stiff airplane seats and having a meaningful conversation with each of them.

The younger man, Wolfgang, falls asleep right away, but Jeff seems eager to talk. When I tell him why I've come to Patmos, he tells me he is a writer too. He gave up a successful life at home to move to Patmos for the solitude and simplicity, he says. Then he tells me that many writers have done the same thing. "In fact," he says, "there's a poet in his seventies living there now who has done quite well in America. His name is Robert Lax."

I can't believe what I've just heard. I tell him about the Merton friend I read about and ask if he thinks it might be the same person. "I'm sure it is," he says. I'm too tired to continue the conversation, but I fall asleep dreaming of meeting Robert Lax.

It's Wolfgang I talk to mostly the next morning. He's from Germany, he tells me, and has spent the past month in a cave preparing to go home to marry. Marriage is a happy surprise for him because he once planned to enter a monastery. He speaks in a tender voice, with a gentle manner, about contemplation in solitude and seeking the face of God, and I wonder how much of his demeanor comes from living humbly in conditions more extreme than mine. What a fortunate woman, I think, to marry a man who prepares himself so seriously and prayerfully for their life together. Our conversation affirms my conviction that solitude is as important for what it prepares us for as for what happens within it.

What does it mean to be blessed? As I disembark from the ferry in Piraeus the next morning, I think of that voice I heard inside while shivering in that doorway. After a month of not talking to anyone about more than the price of groceries, my first conversations are full of meaning and presence. And as I move through the next two weeks, it seems that presence is everywhere, in ways more overt than during my time alone. Conversation after conversation goes beyond the banter travelers usually share and I feel a settledness within me, a comfortableness with my thoughts and beliefs, I didn't feel before my time on Patmos.

The most obvious example comes the day after I spend two nights alone in a youth hostel without heat near the seaside town of Nauplion. While touring the ancient site of Epidaurus on the day between those two nights, I met an Australian couple and we agreed to re-meet at Argos the next morning to travel to Mycenae together. In order to join them on the Mycenae bus, I need to catch a 10 a.m. bus from Nauplion to Argos. But when I wake up and look at my watch, it's already 9:58. I shove my things into my pack, wash my face, and pay for my room as I head out the door. I can flag the bus down on the highway, I think, but the bus doesn't come and it starts to rain, so I trudge into Nauplion to wait for the next one to Argos. I soon learn that it won't be running either and, knowing that strikes are common in Greece, wonder if there's a bus strike on.

When I see a troop carrier full of civilians with a sign for Argos, I ask the soldier next to it if I can ride along, but he tells me no. I try returning to the highway to hitchhike to Argos, but the rain grows heavier and no one even slows. Back at the bus station again, I notice that the area around it is filled with taxis and people are packing into them in groups. Seeing two older women dressed like Americans, I ask if I can ride with them, and they say okay. One has short gray hair and the other longer, slightly darker strands with bangs. They confirm that there's a bus strike on, and when we've chatted amicably for a while, I ask where they're going from Argos. Olympia, they say. Having given up on finding my Australian friends, I ask if I might tag along.

There are no taxis in Argos, so we catch a narrow-gauge train to Tripolis that takes us through a wonderland of hills and valleys as it climbs higher and higher, cutting across steep ravines on single-line bridges. With mist in the valley below, it seems as if we might leave the track at any moment and soar through the air like the car in *Chitty-Chitty-Bang-Bang*. Along the way, I learn that my companions are Georgie, a pastoral counselor from Holland, and Anne, an American Quaker who writes books for disadvantaged children set in housing projects. They met at Yale Divinity School, they tell me, and it's clear from the start that while Georgie is more practical and Anne more metaphysically-oriented, they share a deep but quiet faith.

When we finally make it to Olympia, after a wallet-emptying taxi ride from Tripolis, we find that most of the reasonably-priced hotels are closed for the winter. At the only one still open, the man at the counter tells us he has a three-bed room that would be much cheaper than the two rooms we've asked for. I look at my companions and they look at me and we smile why-not smiles before telling the man we'll take it. As we're setting our luggage down in the room, I wonder out loud what my mother would say if she saw me now. Georgie erupts in laughter.

That night, despite our intention to rise early to see the ancient Olympic site, we sit up on our beds till late talking about theology, counseling, writing, social work, art, and caring for the poor. When I finally put my head to the pillow, I think back to that moment that seems so long ago when I stood in the rain for an hour trying to hitch a ride. *God must have other plans for me today*, I thought as I gave up.

And yet even while I was exulting in my solitude I became aware of a strange lack. I wished a companion to lie near me in the starlight, silent and not moving, but ever within touch. For there is a fellowship more quiet even than solitude, and which, rightly understood, is solitude made perfect.

Robert Louis Stevenson, *Travels with a Donkey in the Cévennes*

A few days later, I board the ferry to return to my solitude on Patmos. In the midst of the coldest and loneliest days on the island, I wrote to my girlfriend in Seattle asking if she'd like to join me for my last two weeks there. When I called her from Athens, she told me no. Sad as her answer made me at first, I have learned in my short life that every no to one thing opens the door to something else. What it will be this time, I don't know, but the first thing I intend to do when I reach the island is look for Robert Lax.

Near the end of my first month on the island, I began to fast once a week from sunup to sundown, as a way of deepening my experience of solitude while also increasing my compassion for those who go hungry every day. Now, as I return, I've embarked on a three-day fast. After indulging myself during my time on the mainland, I want to cleanse my body as well as my mind and spirit. I want to experience the changes in mood and sensation I've read take place when you fast for three or more days. The second day, they say, is the hardest physically, before a "resurrection" on the third day leaves your body feeling better than it's ever felt. The result, they say, is euphoria and clarity in vision.

The first day, on the ferry ride back to Patmos, I feel only a faint headache and a dull hunger. The second day, my feelings run the gamut. One minute I'm reveling in a heightened sense of being alive; the next, I'm feeling so hungry I'm tempted to allow myself a glass of juice. The weakness I feel isn't in my body but in my mind, my will, my spirit. And this is only day two. Again and again in my solitude I've seen how poorly the way I live at home has prepared me for even the slightest hardship. I have to focus on each moment as it comes and move forward through it with thankfulness for it, no matter how I feel.

Once I make it through the second morning, I spend almost all of the rest of the day walking. From the time I step out the door, I feel serene, content, and full of joy. It helps that the sun is shining and spring is clearly coming to Patmos. I can feel it in the breeze and see it in the wildflowers that have already opened. I walk out to Grikou and along the beach, ending up on the monks' rock, where I exchange stares with a lizard before moving on. I don't know if it's just the arrival of spring or if the fasting has enhanced my sense of smell, but the air is charged with wonderful fragrances: the salt of the sea, the perfume of the flowers, the chamomile smell of the open fields. There is a raw physicality to the day, mostly pleasant but at times hard, that keeps my solitude from being ethereal only.

When my walking is done and I return to my apartment, the hunger, dark, and cold sap my motivation. I think of those who face that combination all the time and feel ashamed at how little gratitude I ever feel for the food I consume in abundance at home. One of the goals of my fasting is to fill the time freed from preparing and eating food with gratitude. That was much easier while walking through wildflowers on a sunny day. Once again, I see how different night is from day in solitude. This one, in fact, will end in failure when I wake at 1 a.m. with a headache worse than any I've ever experienced. I cry out to God but the pain persists...until I break my fast with nuts and raisins and aspirin. When the vise grip eases, I fall into a deep sleep, but the whole next day I feel weak and have the sneezing and congestion of a bad cold.

Failure in solitude can be especially frightening: realizing you're not as strong as you believed you were. Fear strikes in weakness or, more accurately, when the mind senses weakness. But failure is a necessary part of solitude. To see ourselves accurately, we need to see our weaknesses as well as our strengths— not only our inadequacies in comparison to others but also the common weakness of being human, animal, alive. Sickness, incapacity, and even death are our constant companions from the day we're born, residing in a shadow self that threatens to become our actual self at any moment.

Even when I'm feeling the joy of being alone, I'm aware that not everyone can choose to be alone in the way I am, and that many are alone without choice, especially the old. This awareness brings a sense of commonality with humanity and the disadvantaged in particular. There is privilege in being able to ignore our weakness, to believe that we are strong and whole alone. There is folly in it too, as anyone who's lost their strength will tell you.

Perhaps it's not entirely a coincidence that the day after my failure at fasting and my feeling of weakness, I find for the first time that I'm not alone. An older Norwegian named Bjorn has moved into the apartment next to mine. His arrival brings a change in my experience on Patmos, from one of total solitude to one of alternation between time alone and companionship.

The evening of his arrival, Bjorn invites me over for a drink and I learn that he is a divorced father of three, a social scientist, and an atheist who chain-smokes rapidly and likes his alcohol. He is also one of the smartest and most knowledgeable people

I've ever met. That first night, starting in his apartment, which is a carbon copy of mine, and continuing in a restaurant in Skala, we eat and drink and talk about everything from the plight of inner-city Blacks in America to the difficulties of cross-cultural marriage. It soon becomes apparent that our views of the world are vastly different. I see it as full of meaning and hope and he sees it as empty of both. I ask what he lives for, then, and he tells me he loves his children. That's all. On the walk back to our apartments, the stars shine brightly above, and when I tell him they're all I need to believe there's something more, he quotes Kant: *Two things fill the mind with ever new and increasing admiration and awe, the more often and steadily we reflect upon them: the starry heavens above me and the moral law within me.*

When we attend an evening service at the Grotto of St. John—a large cave with a roof split into three parts, a rock shelf where the saint supposedly slept, and icons and gold lamps everywhere—Bjorn tells me he hasn't been to a church service in thirty years. The "service" consists of little more than two groups of high school boys singing antiphonally to each other and there isn't much to the grotto itself, but after my month in solitude, it looks different to me than it would have before. I can imagine the struggles, pains, and fears the exiled John must have gone through in order to experience and record his visions.

The only other service I attend in those days, I attend alone. It comes on a day I take my camera to the monks' rock at Grikou to take pictures and, as usual, the pup I've nicknamed Gabriel joins me. When I'm done with the rock, I follow him as if he truly is an angel and he leads me into a heavenly land of field after field of wildflowers. As I photograph them, I take the time (since I have it) to carefully look at each one, and I find there are dozens of varieties thrown together like immigrants at a border crossing. I take pictures of only the most outstanding ones and still I record a dozen kinds. Every time I think an iris or poppy

I've just photographed will be the last, Gabriel leads me on to an even more glorious hillside, until we come to nirvana: a field of white daises dotted with orange crepe-paper flowers that seems to stretch to the end of the earth. The sun is low in the sky by now and everywhere the colors are brilliant: the sea a deep blue, a farmhouse bright white, fields beyond it lustrous green. If there is a heaven, I think, I know now what to expect.

From there, I walk with Gabriel up through the cooling twilight toward Chora. As we near the monastery, the bells ring out and, although I'm tired and hungry, I enter the complex to see what's happening. The courtyard is gently lit, its peacefulness accentuated by strains of soft chanting floating out from the church the caretaker points me to. The walls of the church are covered with disintegrating frescoes, with wooden structures with fold-down seats in front of them. After lighting a candle, I sit in a corner on one of the wooden seats to watch the black-robed monks chant back and forth before their God. The church is filled with the scent of incense, and several times the crimson-robed monk holding the censer passes in front of me. Each time I bow and he "anoints" me. As in the grotto, icons and lamps are everywhere, but the light shines only where it's needed and the candles cast a solemn glow against blackened walls and arches. Monks take turns looking at me as if I'm a vagabond they should send away or maybe an apparition of Christ, as their tradition says any stranger might be. I stare right back at them, examining their uncut beards and the carefully pinned-up hair below their black, pot-like hats.

At first an older woman and I are the only ones there, but then a family arrives and, when what I assume is a sermon starts, I slip out into the fresh night air. Before I descend toward Skala, I pause on the monastery steps and gaze at a myriad of stars in the black sky above. "Thank you, God," I say, "for a day lived in paradise." When I finally put my feet to the hill, Gabriel is nowhere in sight, but one more angel appears: a man stopping his car to give me a ride.

I set these descriptions down in a book on solitude not only because I was alone that day but also because the solitude I'd already experienced increased my awareness—and enjoyment—of every flower and smell and lamplight and ritual.

If solitude has a season in the Christian calendar, it has to be Advent or maybe Lent, a time of contemplation and preparation that has a meaning independent of what it leads to. During my time in solitude, I had no expectations. Even though it was winter, I didn't think of the coming spring or hope for eventual blessing. I was there to work and watch and learn who I was. So a day like the one I spent with Gabriel wasn't the point or the goal; I wasn't there in pursuit of happiness. Yet happiness came, and I was able to see more clearly the blessing it was because of what I'd done. As beautiful as that blessing was, however, it paled in comparison to what I was about to experience.

The best remedy for those who are afraid, lonely or unhappy is to go outside, somewhere where they can be quite alone with the heavens, nature and God. Because only then does one feel that all is as it should be and that God wishes to see people happy amidst the simple beauty of nature. As long as this exists, and it certainly always will, I know that then there will always be comfort for every sorrow, whatever the circumstances may be.

Anne Frank, *The Diary of a Young Girl*

I don't know how to find Robert Lax, even on a small island, so I ask the only person I've talked with—Anna at the grocery store—if she knows a man called Petros, the name Jeff told me the islanders use for Lax. To my delight, she says he visits her store every day. I ask her to let him know I'm looking for him and she says she will, but when I check with her the following day, she tells me he hasn't come in. The same is true the next day. And the next. Finally, on the fourth day, she says she saw him. He told her to tell me he goes to the post office at 10 a.m. each day.

I've already described my first meeting with Lax in my biography of him, *Pure Act: The Uncommon Life of Robert Lax*, so I'll focus here on what knowing I'll soon be face-to-face with Merton's friend does to me. That night, I can't sleep. I try reading an academic book on the Bolshevik revolution, but even that doesn't tire me out. So I lie awake, listening to a neighbor's rooster, and then write an ode to him, celebrating the restless state that keeps us both up. Before long, I see the light through the shutters reflecting off the ceiling and open the window to greet the day. When 10 a.m. rolls around, it has started to rain and no one on Patmos goes out in the rain, but I trudge down to the post office anyway and, when Lax isn't there, leave a note asking him to meet me at a nearby taverna at 6 p.m. Then I drowse away the rest of the day between peals of thunder, wondering if he'll come.

That evening, to my great delight, he appears, and I know as soon as I see him that he is Merton's Lax. I tell him right away what I thought when I heard he was on the island: that God had something for him to tell me or me to tell him. As it turns out, we have things to tell each other. We end up meeting every night for the rest of my stay on the island, and as we chat in his small house above Skala, it begins to seem, above all, that we were simply meant to be friends.

Of all of the gifts Lax gave me over the fifteen years I would know him before his death in 2000, one of the greatest came right away. As I've said, moving to Patmos was an experiment, an attempt to see if living a creative life was for me. By the end of my month alone, I'd decided not only that it was but also that solitude had to be part of it, as well as a turning away from the expectations and strivings of "normal" American life. I didn't know, however, if living a life outside those expectations and strivings could be done—if one could live fully, simply, and joyfully at the same time. Witnessing the way Lax lived in his small house on a remote island and seeing that he, at sixty-nine, was not only kind, creative, intelligent, and spiritually aware but also full of humor and joy, made me believe it was possible to cross the difficult waters of middle life with your simplicity, creativity, faith, and even innocence intact.

Even today, forty years later, I think of Lax every day. I think of the solitude in which he lived and the insights, blessings, and poems that came out of it. I think of an evening shortly after we met when he said to me, "Wherever you go, wherever you are, have a place where you can be alone for contemplation and time with God." That same evening, he quoted the Buddhist monk Thich Nhat Hanh: "People say, 'Don't just sit there, do something.' I say, 'Don't just do something, sit there.'"

Time after time, when I said something Lax liked, he told me, "Write it down." Your beliefs are good and strongly held, he'd say, and that's how they should be written. Write what you know and what you mean. And do it for yourself alone. Don't write for publication or to make money. Write what you have to say and then find someone who will publish it. Your true thoughts will find their way onto the page more clearly that way, and that's the real goal.

My talks with Lax send my mind twirling and somersaulting in new directions. One night when my departure from the island is imminent, we talk about dreams. When I tell him about the ones I've had during my time in solitude, he tells me to write those down too. That night, of course, I have a vivid one and fill five notebook pages with it. The following night—my last on the island—I have that dream about dancing in the church.

The blessedness of learning ever more about myself while

living alone with two extraordinary friends nearby is making me realize I've found a new mistress: solitude. I was acquainted with her when I was a child but I was too young to savor her charms. Now she offers an alluring alternative to the life I've been living. I wonder, though, if she can survive beside a flesh-and-blood partner.

Lax never married and I see countless similarities between us. Am I a person, I wonder, who can go through life alone? Or is there a woman somewhere who can live out Rilke's definition of love with me: *two solitudes that meet, protect and greet each other*?

As vibrantly felt as it is vividly imagined, sense of place asserts itself at varying levels of mental and emotional intensity. Whether it is lived in memory or experienced on the spot, the strength of its impact is commensurate with the richness of its contents, with the range and diversity of symbolic associations that swim within its reach and move it on its course.

Keith H. Basso, *Wisdom Sits in Places*

My final day on the island I wake up at the secret hour of 4 a.m. to record my dream of dancing in the church and open the shutters for one last look at the stars above Patmos. The endless lights and the glow they throw like a glaze over everything make the sky and the land look unreal. The Milky Way is milkier than I've ever seen it, a Broadway running through the center of our galaxy. I don't know that I will ever find myself again in the right place and time to see the stars so bright. By the time I've recorded the dream, the morning light is painting the heavens, and the fields are turning a brilliant green, as if a window shade has been lifted. Instead of getting up, I linger in my wool socks with my wrapping of blanket, moving from dreams to poems and feeling, although I haven't left it yet, nostalgic for Patmos. I hear the children at the nearby school and watch the crows fly and want to sit like this forever.

When I told Lax I'd begun to notice the way crows move and been amazed they could stay suspended with nothing but air to hold them up, he said he'd noticed the same thing on Patmos. "The birds are more relaxed here," he said, "and because of how they fly, the wonder of flight itself is more apparent." His words are consistent with how I've come to view Patmos in general: as a magical land where everyone and everything is touched by the magic.

Before I move, I close my eyes and thank God for all of life. Then I shower and eat and do a final washing of clothes before I set out with my camera to capture a few last images. It is March 25, Annunciation Day in the Catholic Church but more importantly Greek Independence Day here. The sun is out and warm and when I see cars full of people in their Sunday best moving up the hill toward Chora, I follow them. At the top, I find monks in black robes, military men in full dress uniform, and children in traditional costumes parading toward the grave of the island's liberator. When they reach it, they place wreathes on the gravestone to commemorate the war that freed them from the Ottoman yoke two hundred years ago.

Continuing down the other side of the hill, I find another field of wildflowers and snap pictures of the blossoms and a black-and-yellow honeybee armed with leg sacks of bright orange pollen. Down in a valley that ends in the sea, I hear the tinkle of goat bells near a trickling stream. For the first time, the goats don't seem disturbed at my approach and I stop among them to watch a mother nursing her young, a billy goat nibbling grass, and a cluster of frolicking youngsters who peer at me with curiosity. When one comes near and I lower my hand to rub its head, I hear shouts from the farmhouse below. I think at first the people there might be angry at me for disturbing their animals, but then I see them waving me down. Soon, I'm "conversing" with two old men and an older woman without a shared language. The woman brings me a cup of Greek coffee and a very welcome glass of water and there in the hot sun we celebrate independence together, without a breath of sound drifting in from outside the valley.

Before I leave, they ask in mime if I'm going to swim and I tell them, laughing, the water is still too cold. But when I'm on my own again, I change my mind. Looking for an ideal place to immerse myself, I pass through a cleft in the rocks and gaze down on yet another vision of paradise. The water washes over large smooth stones, a bright aquamarine, and cliffs rise all around to shut out the world. Soon, I'm slipping off my clothes and plunging into the Aegean's cooling waters. Other than quick baths on hikes in wilderness at home, I've never skinny-dipped before. Perhaps this is my Independence Day too, I think. A freeing of myself from my own yoke. After my swim, I lie naked on the rocks and fall asleep in the warm air, a sinless solitary child of God. Only when I have dressed and am climbing back up the cliff do I realize that the convent I saw on one of my earlier walks is directly above.

I stop again at the top of Chora's hill and gaze out over the island one last time. What was once a blank slate is now a map of my experiences. I have made Patmos my own.

When I tell Bjorn what I've been doing, he says, "Ah, you're still young enough for such things." I chat with him a while and then head out for another walk: my last before I catch the ferry. The air is cool against my arms and sunburned face as I descend the road I've walked so many times with Buby. Just beyond the hotel where the men watched movies in winter, I breathe the scent of orange blossoms, and when I see Buby tied up in my landlord's yard I go over to pet him. He strains against his chain, wanting to join me, and I feel sad leaving him behind, especially since I won't see him again.

Although I'd love to climb up into one of the caves at Grikou once more, I have time only for a visit to the little beach where I imagined pixies dancing. As I stare out at the sea and shoreline, I think of a night when I sat there in the depths of the cold and felt the longings of Adam for "flesh of my flesh." Now I think I'd be a fool to exchange the serenity of solitude for anything or anyone.

My last stop before I return to my apartment for my pack and typewriter is at Lax's place. After my time on the beach, I don't feel like talking, but over a plate of giant beans he gets me laughing with tales of his days in Hollywood, including a description of Groucho Marx riding by in a long sleek limousine. For once, we don't talk about anything deep, either because we think there will be more time in the future or because this is our last time together and we won't be able to finish any discussion we begin. After eating, we walk the road to my apartment, where I introduce him to Bjorn for the first time and they chat as I pack the last of my things. Then the three of us make our way to the harbor. As I breathe in the scent of the orange blossoms once more, I realize that even if I walk that road again, it will never hold all it's held for me this visit.

We settle into a café by the water, but this time the wait for the ferry is short. Before I'm ready for it, I'm entering the bowels of the *Ialyssos*, having said goodbye to what seem in that moment to be my only friends in the world. When I find my way to the rear deck and look out into the glow of the boat's lights, Lax is already gone. But there at the edge of the crowd I see Bjorn. When I whistle, he turns. I know he knows it's me who whistled, but his half-blind eyes can't find me. I wave anyway. And as the ferry moves away, I watch my friend through bleary eyes. Faithful friend, I think. Faithful land. I ask myself if I will ever return, but I know before the question is fully formed that I will. I must.

When the other passengers have all left the deck, I stay and watch the lights of Chora recede into the night. Then I take my harmonica out and play "Loch Lomond." It's the first tune I learned on the harmonica. The one I played in that cave at Grikou. The one I sang as I wandered the island's paths and, one night, with Bjorn. I play it now, with all my missed notes and awkward timing, as a kind of final goodbye—to a friend and a time and a place I've loved.

A place belongs forever to whoever claims it hardest, remembers it most obsessively, wrenches it from itself, shapes it, renders it, loves it so radically that he remakes it in his own image.

Joan Didion, *The White Album*

Reincarnations
(1985-1989)

TAIZÉ

Let silence take you to the core of life.

_____

Rumi

O ver the seven months that follow my time on Patmos, I'm
rarely alone again. After spending April with a friend in
Egypt and Israel, I stay with my mother for two months in her
tiny condo while making up for lost time with my girlfriend and
working for the American travel writer Rick Steves in preparation
for leading tours for him in the summer. It seems I've barely been
home when I fly back over to Europe for the first of three three-
week excursions, during which I'm with people day and night.

When the last tour ends, I'm so exhausted and anxious and
out of touch with myself I don't know what to do next. Instead of
resting, though, or acting on the desire for solitude I've written
about in my journal, I drift up to Scandinavia and back to Paris,
visiting friends, meeting strangers, taking night trains to save
time and money. By this time my girlfriend and I have broken
up and the only thing that slackens my lust for new sights and
experiences is the mention by two people of a place in southern

France dedicated to spiritual contemplation. Their descriptions alone are like the distant call of a beloved voice, pleading with me to stop what I'm doing and catch a train south.

After all of my traveling, nothing is easier than falling asleep on a moving conveyance. When I wake up this time, the train is clicking through a dreamland of rolling hills and farmland lit, between shadows, by a welcome sun. My mind is still hazy from my nap when the conductor announces my destination, Mâcon, and I emerge into the easy warmth of Burgundy. After orienting myself at the station, I find my way to the road to Cluny, the medieval town whose Benedictine abbey dominated European monasticism in the eleventh and twelfth centuries. I've been reading Umberto Eco's *The Name of the Rose*, so my mind is already filled with monks and chants and medieval settings. My destination, Taizé, isn't far from Cluny—and Cluny isn't far from Mâcon—but I've been told there's no easy way to reach it unless you have a car. So, as soon as I find the right road, I stick out my thumb.

I've been so busy for so long, even standing alone in the late-day sun as cars whiz by calms my soul. Eventually, a Citroën deux chevaux slows to a stop beside me. The woman behind the wheel is blond and maybe ten years older than me. She smiles and invites me in and soon we're cruising along through the bright afternoon with endless fields around us. Although we don't share a common language, she asks somehow if I've ever been to the area and when I say no she turns up a road to show me a stone church and then the local castle. The combination of kindness and quiet and amber light soothes the franticness from my being. When she leaves me on the side of the road on the outskirts of Cluny, I feel prepared for the week ahead.

I still have several kilometers to go, however, so I stick my thumb out again. This time the ride I get is with three raucous Frenchmen and two children who chatter and laugh and honk as they drop me off at Taizé with shouts of *au revoir* and *bon chance*. Like a scherzo after a quiet movement, their revelry is unsettling at first, but as I watch them drive away I realize my soul is filled with that perfect combination of peacefulness and good humor.

After checking in, I wander a rural road in the early dusk past stone walls and empty fields that seem straight out of Eco's medieval world. When I circle back, I hear the sound of soft music coming from the large plain building with the onion dome I've learned is called the Church of Reconciliation. Inside, I find an open space enclosed by plywood walls without pews or chairs or anything else except a few icons here and there. The lighting comes only from hanging lamps and a few candles where an altar might be. The room is already filling with people my age or younger, and as the music continues to play, white-robed men with thrown-back hoods file in, two-by-two, and sit, with everyone else, on the bare floor. As the gentle singing shifts and blends with Bible passages and prayers spoken through a microphone, I sit by myself in the back and feel the peace enter me like a silent fog. Meet me here, I pray. Speak to me. Settle me. Love me.

All I really know about Taizé is that it calls itself ecumenical and caters primarily to the young. I will learn in the days ahead that it was started by a Swiss man known as Brother Roger who bought a house in the area in 1940 with the intention of serving the needs of wartime refugees. Eventually, other young men gathered around him and they formed a community together. In the 1960s, young people searching for meaning beyond their parents' world discovered them and, attracted to their blend of simple songs and quiet prayer, began to hang around. As more and more young people arrived, the brothers decided to treat them like refugees too, providing them with simple housing and food and caring for their spiritual and emotional needs. Now, groups and individuals come from across Europe to be cared for in this way.

My intention is to stay for only a week, not as a way of seeking solitude, but simply to be with people my age in a spiritual setting free from the trappings of traditional churches. I've never sought out a retreat center before and I like that this one doesn't have a structured program designed to "enlighten" me in some way. The brothers seem to trust that a peaceful orientation toward God is enough.

The organizers assign me to a group and give me a task for the week: babysitting the children of other visitors. The brothers host a daily session in which we discuss issues the world faces, but for me the week consists mostly of interacting with playful children, wandering the fields, and attending peaceful prayers. One day I learn it's possible to stay a second week in silence. Wanting to give myself more completely to the spirit of the place, I sign up. This is a chance, I think, to stay in community without the burden of having to speak. To enter a kind of solitude without being solitary.

"This is a time to allow God to fill the silence with his presence," a monk named Brother Emile tells us on our first silent morning. "It's not a time to catch up on letter writing or book reading." I know he's right, but my impulse is to do the things I did on Patmos. Instead, I sit on my single room's small porch and watch the sun disperse the mists in the valley. A choir of birds sings around me and I thank God birds never go into silence.

Others from the week before have chosen silence too, and I quickly realize how strong the impulse is to speak when we see people we know. As the impulse lessens, however, being quiet with people nearby begins to feel freeing. My job for this week is ferrying food into the dining hall and I feel free to just enjoy it and the sun without words interfering.

More importantly, silence frees me to truly look at others, to watch how they do what they do and think about it. For example, as I watch a younger man who was with me the first week consume a cookie, I notice he bites into it without breaking it into smaller pieces as I do. When I was a Boy Scout, I always wondered why adults on hikes sliced their apples up with a knife when it was easier to bite into them. I wonder now if the difference has something to do with age. A child takes a bite from the whole and, if it comes apart in some way, deals with what happens. An adult, on the other hand, partitions things to control them, fearing that jumping in might lead to unforeseen consequences.

The only person I talk with that second week is Brother Emile, a thin, pleasant Canadian-American who comes to my room each day at 4. Mostly all we do is talk, but he also gives me a Bible passage each day to guide my reflections. One is Psalm 16, which says in part: "my flesh also shall rest in hope." When I dare to talk about sexual desires, Brother Emile tells me God doesn't deny our natural inclinations, but rather transfigures them. This idea is so different from the condemnation of physical feelings I heard from the pulpit of my childhood church, it leads to a discussion of passion and celibacy. For the first time, I contemplate embracing solitude entirely by joining a community or monastic order that features it. So many elements of a quieter life suit me. What my contemplation shows me, however, is that my desires aren't so simple. While silence and stability appeal to me, so do the beauty and variety in the world, including the beauty of talking with people unlike me, traveling through unknown places, and seeking intimacy with another earthly soul. As I did on Patmos, I feel drawn to two seemingly contradictory desires: being entirely alone with God and being fully present with others, especially a companion who is "flesh of my flesh."

Another part of Psalm 16 says: "The lines are fallen unto me in pleasant places; yea, I have a goodly heritage." This one speaks so strongly to me, I take up the brush and paints I find in my room and paint a picture of it, with green fields under blue skies, using the wool I find on the barbs of nearby fences to fashion plump sheep. What it means to me is that the life I'm living is fine as it is, with all of its blessings and yearnings and even uncertainties. All I need is time apart now and then for quiet reflection.

Without books or a project like the novel I wrote on Patmos, I expect my week alone in silence to pass slowly, but in fact it passes more quickly than other weeks. In the absence of distractions, sitting quietly alone becomes immensely pleasant. I watch a pheasant fly only for me, a hedgehog pause as if to chat, and field mice scurry away, wanting nothing to do with me. On my last night of solitude without being solitary, I sit in the church in silence for several hours, feeling free of the physical struggles of being young while simply existing in the warm, quiet light with the gentle singing. If I have learned anything this week other than how to quiet my soul, it's that I don't have to absent myself entirely to receive the benefits of solitude. In fact, silence in community can yield perspectives and insights total seclusion can't.

ROTHENBURG-OB-DER-TAUBER

I restore myself when I'm alone.

Marilyn Monroe

In this most touristed of towns in what is still West Germany, I sit alone in the evening light in what is called the Castle Garden, the area just outside the medieval walls where the old fortress foundations have been turned into a park. The colors haven't drained yet from the nearby buildings; in fact, they grow more intense with each passing moment, as if they know they'll soon die and so live all the more fully. A man I've seen in the park before, in the dark below a full moon, is playing a violin beside the watchtower. Flowers of red, yellow, pink, and white huddle together, their faces turned toward nearby trees as if afraid of the coming winter. Japanese tourists in fashionable clothes play games with each other, and two people from my group stroll by without seeing me. They are a happy group, trusting and laughing, and they make me happy too. I earn my living now by leading tours, and when the group is good I like to be with it. But tonight, I'm pensive—not sad but feeling the fullness of life.

Sometimes the loveliness is too much for me. I don't want to lose it. Can't the grass's greenness remain? I think. Must the flowers die? Can't this woman near me, with her graying hair, continue to be young inside? I can't accept that one day the violin will be silent and the pretty women will pass me by without a glance. I hope to always have a castle garden to retire to, at sunset when the day has left its mark, content with what it offered.

As the violin plays on, a man sets up his canvas and begins to paint. Two German boys stand yards apart and throw sticks toward one another. What pleases me is their abandonment to each other, the silliness it allows, the respect of friendship that makes total enjoyment of and by another possible. The game is unimportant; the expression of one's self is all. They are happy because they've allowed themselves and each other to be. A bell tolls somewhere and the sun slips down below the trees. Soon the color will be gone and I will have to leave to find my group.

I never intended to become a tour guide, but working for Rick Steves provides a decent income and there are so many places I still want to see. I spend more time in Europe now than at home. When I'm on tour, I wake up early to join the group for breakfast; sit up front in a large bus and point out sights along the way; arrange lunches; give tours through museums; offer music and games to keep my clients entertained; assign rooms at the end of the day; and join the group again for dinner, which often leads to evening events, planned or spontaneous. On some tours, I'm with tour members seventeen or eighteen hours a day for three straight weeks.

On the last day of the first tour I led by myself, as I lay in my Paris room with the windows open on a hot afternoon, I heard a couple bitching about me across the courtyard. I'd given all I had and was exhausted. I didn't think I'd ever lead another tour. But I needed money and I wasn't going to let one apparent failure defeat me, so I signed up for another summer. When the next tour came along, instead of trying to follow someone else's example, I led it my way, which included taking time for myself, like this evening in the Castle Garden.

Most days, I give the group the same free time I give myself and they're happier for it. Of course, they're happier, in part, because I'm more fully myself and therefore better at guiding. The main tour I lead runs from Amsterdam down to Germany, along the Rhine, to Rothenburg, Mad King Ludwig's Neuschwanstein Castle, a rural town called Reutte in Austria, and Innsbruck, before we cross the border into Italy. There, when we've visited the big three—Venice, Rome, and Florence—we spend two nights by the sea in the Cinqueterre before climbing into the Swiss Alps, crossing to the medieval Alsatian town of Colmar, and finishing in Paris.

Most of my solitude along the way comes in two-hour chunks during which I sit somewhere with my journal and write down thoughts and observations. The particular thoughts I set down are less important than the act, the pleasure, and the refreshment that comes from pulling into myself for those few minutes. Eventually, I have a favorite place everywhere I have any time for myself: the Castle Garden in Rothenburg; a restaurant on the back of the hill at Neuschwanstein; a hidden café behind the old ramparts on the Cinqueterre; an isolated bench with a view of the Eiger, the Mönch, and the Jungfrau on an empty trail in the Alps. In Rothenburg, the Cinqueterre, and Switzerland, I sometimes have an entire day to wander by myself. None of these times are long enough to enter into the kind of solitude I experienced on Patmos or even at Taizé, but they give me space and quiet to rest my spirit enough to keep going.

There are a hundred reasons to seek solitude. The most profound, I suppose, is to find enlightenment or hear the voice of God, like Moses, Buddha, Jesus, and Mohammed. Hindu swamis seek solitude in pursuit of mastering themselves. Writers and other artists seek it in order to concentrate exclusively on their writing or painting or music. John Muir sought it to find beauty and fresh air. The most basic reason people seek solitude, however, is rest. Recuperation. Especially in our work-obsessed Western world.

Of course, we all enter a kind of recuperative solitariness every time we go to sleep. And most of us, when we're truly weary, are quick to say, like Greta Garbo, *I want to be alone.* But sleep and even time alone in which we're too tired to do much of anything aren't truly solitude. Important as they are, they can't offer the tonic to the spirit that a chosen time away from others and from distractions does.

When I can, I take a week off between tours, not just to rest or recover but also to refill my being. If I'm going to spend three weeks giving everything I have to others, I need to be full when I start. Full of what, you might ask. A sense of myself. A sense of what's important. A sense of the glory of being alive. If I feel fully alive, if I feel loved because I'm living in the presence of God, if I feel wonder at the world around me, I have something to offer others. In the end, the most valuable thing we can give to another person is life, and life comes most readily from a feeling of being fully present. Fully human. Fully connected to the world and its inhabitants. It is because of this fullness that we can love. That we know the meaning of love.

One thing I learn from leading tours and traveling on my own between them is that places of solitude can be found everywhere. One day, while away from my group in the Alps, I take a cable car to a place called Alpenhubel, a bald hill used for skiing in winter and to access the heights for hiking in summer. It's September and the sun is out. Instead of hiking, however, I find a bench and just sit, and soon my hillside turns fascinating. A man in a kilt and cap lingers with his Scottish companion, and a German man with a movie camera chats amorously with a plump, attractive French girl young enough to be his daughter. Off in the distance I notice a hawk wheeling out over the valley. As it circles closer, everyone looks up to watch it, transfixed by its upturned wings, the unflinching pride of its lifted beak. For a moment, we are all one—the bird, the hillside, and the humans—and then the moment is gone. The French girl says goodbye. The German wanders off. The Scots settle down to their picnic lunch. And I am left with an image that would not be mine if I hadn't lingered there alone. I am alive, I say to myself. Wonderfully alive.

Once, when I feel unusually exhausted between tours, I take a room with a tiny window on the river in Trier and spend a week sleeping and wandering around the town without talking to anyone. Another time, intrigued by a line in my *Michelin Guide*, I travel high up in the Swiss Alps and stay in a youth hostel annex where an older French couple are the only other occupants. Every day, they go one way and I go another, and when we meet in the evening in the common room where we eat our supper, we talk about our day. There are no sights except mountains. There's nothing to do except move through the natural world. Yet every night, when we meet, we have more to say than we have time for, they from their solitude and I from mine. We don't just talk about things we've seen; we talk about what they've stirred inside us: previous experiences, things we've read, ideas we haven't thought about in years, all given new and interesting twists by questions we ask each other, questions we explore together, questions so big they have no answers but give us something to think about while on our own the next day.

Because most of the tours I lead end in Paris, I spend much of my solitude there. Eventually, I come to know it better than any city other than my hometown of Seattle. Cities are thought to be lonely places but they can be excellent places to find solitude, especially foreign ones where you don't speak the language. You can wander at will for days with life around you but nothing to disturb your thoughts, your feelings, your awareness. This is especially true in a city as dynamic and human-scaled as Paris, as long as you leave the guidebook in your room.

Sometimes in Paris I go to new museums and stand alone in front of great art for as long as it takes me to learn from what I'm seeing—not about technique but about life itself. I draw from the intersecting of what the artist has created and what's inside me. Only when I'm alone can that intersecting take place.

My favorite place to be alone while traveling in Europe is on trains. I take a seat by the window and write or read or simply watch the scenery go by. Although I can understand some French and German and Italian, unless English speakers sit near me, I'm able to tune out what's being said. My knowledge of other languages is pleasingly rudimentary. If I don't pay attention, even words I know fly by without me recognizing them, leaving me in my own bubble. Traveling by train allows me to be still and still moving—to sink into my inner world while being immersed in a changing outer one.

PATMOS

Knowing how to be solitary is central to the art of loving. When we can be alone, we can be with others without using them as a means of escape.

bell hooks, *All About Love: New Visions*

I see the lights of Chora floating in the nighttime sky and think of my first return a year ago, when I crossed the ferry from side to side searching for them, like a dog in a family car nearing home. They still seemed magical then. Beacons from a mythic land. Now, they bring no joy. No wonder. The harbor light beams out its welcome, the hotel sign beckons me, but I feel nothing. My first return, I brought a friend and regretted it immediately. *Patmos is a place to be alone*, I thought and left as soon as I could. Now, the loneliness of being on my own after months of leading tours and traveling with strangers—schmoozing and reveling and losing touch with who I am—is too much for me.

For weeks, now, I've been drifting along, trying to decide whether to return home and settle for a more conventional life—a regular job, maybe marriage—or move to Europe—Patmos, in particular—and risk the lessened ties to friends and family. The drifting and deliberating have left me feeling useless, guilty, and, above all, scared. What I need is what I fear: time alone. Time to look at myself and my life honestly.

When I've dropped my bag at the Hotel Rex, I take the road that leads uphill toward the monastery, the older road built long ago of hewn stone, weathered and uneven. Just above where I used to live, I find a section of the old wall where the stone is smooth and almost level. There, I lie below the midnight sky and gaze at stars that haven't beamed so bright since I was last here. I find the Pleiades and the Big Dipper, and watch a shooting star gash a tear in the black curtain. I try to pray but words won't come. Instead, a jumbled clot of feelings, needs, and intimations rises through the silent air.

As I stare at all those points of light, the immensity of what we call the universe strikes me. Are those really suns with worlds around them? I wonder. Am I really worth the fuss I make about myself? The lines of a psalm come to mind: *When I look at thy heavens, the work of thy fingers, the moon and the stars which thou hast established; what is man that thou art mindful of him, and the son of man that thou doth care for him? Yet thou hast made him little less than God...*

Lying undisturbed like this is what a place like Patmos gives me. Time that is both time and not-time. Time unpromised to people or activities. Time still undefined, unassigned, unburdened by what seemed the heaviest load moments ago. As I lie with beaming stars above, the emotions that seemed so dire when I lay down begin to fade or clarify. What seems clearest of all is that I have an intense need to be loved both by God and in a nurturing relationship with flesh and blood—that I am, in equal measures, spirit and body. And yet the right relationship has eluded me so far.

My old friend Lax says that Western society is preoccupied with the body, babying it with labor-saving devices and the latest medicines and creams, while neglecting the spiritual and creative side. Although I agree, I think I feel my own embodiment more keenly than he does. I know I'll never become what he has become: a solitary man with social connections. I'll always be a social man who needs solitude. Therefore, solitude is different for him than for me. He is a fish and I am an otter. He exists in solitude, absorbing it through gills intended for it, while I remain adjacent to it, dipping in from time to time to swim around. For a while, I can live exclusively in solitude or society—each, in its own way, sustains me—but eventually I crave what I don't have, and the transition from one to the other is always painful.

Central to the pain is fear. When I have been alone and come to know myself again, I feel more whole and real than in society. But I emerge more vulnerable—like a turtle hatchling lacking a carapace. From the moment I reappear, it seems society is out to challenge, shape, adulterate what I've discovered. Indifference, insensitivity, casual cruelty, and outright spite eat away my peace of mind. My fortitude. My humanity. Yet society is where I know I have access to love—both the love of others and the love inside myself. In society I have opportunities to give. To listen. To heal. It's primarily that love that makes it difficult to pull away. But in this age of constant contact, it's also stimulation, entertainment, and casual connection that substitutes for the real thing. Without my realizing it, my soul loses its dimensions, its flavor, its depth. It becomes a flattened roll of unbaked dough headed for the cookie cutter. It's then I need to get away. But painful as it was to re-enter society, it's even more painful to leave it. Suddenly, every meaningless connection seems vital and the solitude my soul craves a frightening void. Only the promise of presence— God's and my own—gives me the courage to enter a darkness that looks to be as endless as night but is only a thin veil. A brief transition.

By the time I lift myself off the wall, I feel the calm assurance of a different love, a universal love manifested in the stars, the stillness, the soft scent of the cultivated land. The fear and loneliness I felt as I approached Patmos have begun to ebb away. Not for good, perhaps, but for now. As I walk back toward my room, I remember a line from the Merton book I was reading on the ferry: *Wherever we go, we discover that [God] has just arrived before us.*

The next day is Thanksgiving back home. Having found

my old landlord and rented my former apartment again, I buy a chicken at the store and boil it to eat with mashed potatoes and peas, approximating the feast I'd be eating with my family. I remember another time I was alone on this day, traveling in England. Tired and feeling sick, I stepped into a church where a boys' choir was practicing sacred songs in Gothic glory. Taking a seat in the back of the empty sanctuary, I closed my eyes and rested in their heavenly harmonies.

It was on that same trip, maybe that same night, I turned the television on in my bed-and-breakfast and caught the end of an American Western. I watched as an Indian man delivered a horse to a white man at his home. The white man tried to refuse the gift but the Indian insisted he keep it. When the white man asked if he could at least give the Indian a ride home, the man replied, "The walk is part of the gift." That snippet from an otherwise forgettable film has always stuck with me, as a reminder not to do the minimum for others but to give until the giving becomes sacrifice. I like to think the solitude of the walk home deepened that giver's sense of what he'd done.

Later that Thanksgiving evening, I walk down to the ferry dock to wait for Lax, who has told me by letter he'll return on that night's boat. When he sees me, he hugs me warmly and insists I accompany him to his house to share the evening meal he knows his neighbor has prepared for him. Although a year and a half have passed, it seems there's been no lapse in our conversation. In fact, it seems our thinking has been traveling down the same paths. He shows me a paragraph he clipped from a recent issue of the *International Herald Tribune*, a quote from philosopher William James: "I have often thought that the best way to define a man's character would be to seek out the particular mental or moral attitude in which, when it came upon him, he felt himself most deeply and intensely active and alive. At such moments there is a voice inside which speaks and says: 'This is the real me!'" I tell him I tore out the same paragraph. In this moment, on this island of solitude, it seems he's the real him and I'm the real me.

Before I leave, we talk about something I read in his friend Merton's book that meshed with my own thoughts: when we pursue what is necessary for us to be most fully alive, whether that is mere solitude or writing in solitude or some other imaginative activity, we do it not only for ourselves but also for others and for God, for we cannot give ourselves fully to others if we are not fully present. "It's that old idea," Lax says, "of being alone for others."

That night I sleep poorly and dream, as I dreamed my first time on Patmos. This time, though, my dreams are full of negative images, including someone being stabbed in the stomach. They are evidence to me that whatever has lodged inside me during weeks of ignoring my interior life will take time to pass away. To be cleaned out.

These kinds of dreams are part of solitude too. As we go through our days, we all accumulate images, emotions, and half-formed thoughts. We absorb the looks others give us, good and bad, and our bodies react to what we put in them, whether it's food or drink or unintended messages from pop culture, including misogyny, racism, and violence. Unless we take the time to contemplate and filter what we consume, the residues of all these things lodge in us like the apple in the shell of Kafka's beetle, rotting there until we work them out. Solitude can be a cleanser, but cleansing takes time, and so the first moments or even days alone can bring disturbing thoughts and images.

It's those things that have lodged in me—and what it means that I've let them—that cause much of the fear I feel in being alone. I'm afraid to face them. To confront my complicity in letting them disturb my life. To admit that they've caused me to live fearfully among others. I'm afraid to look at myself, as I truly am—the tendency to drink too much on tours, the lustfulness that substitutes for meaningful connection, the callousness and impatience I often express to those who are closest to me—without averting my eyes. And I'm afraid of being alone with God without an intercessor—not the loving God whose presence I desire or even the God portrayed by some as seeking retribution, but the God of fairness and justice and mercy who will find me wanting. It isn't punishment or even judgment I fear; it's a fair assessment of how I've been living. What I've pursued. The good work I've left undone.

When I stop in to see Lax the next day, he talks to me about moments—not past moments or future moments but present moments, this moment: this pinpoint of time in which our lives intersect with eternity. In every moment, he says, we make choices, decisions, large and small. True life comes from understanding that these decisions are of ultimate importance. His words remind me of the line from Baba Ram Dass that seemed the essence of life when I heard it in a college class at nineteen: *Be here now.* Consciousness—presentness—is what the current moment demands, a state of existence more easily remembered and acted upon in solitude.

Among the books I've brought along this time is Anne Morrow Lindbergh's *Gift from the Sea,* in which she writes of moments in regard to love. There are moments of love that exist only for themselves, she says, and there are moments of love that lead on to deeper moments. In my travels, I've encountered only the first kind. Only in solitude on Patmos do I experience the second: a deeper well of goodness and faith and empathy inside me, one I know will be with me until the end of my days, even when I fail to recognize it.

One day, before visiting Lax, I wander out along the high ridge just behind his house, where I've found pottery remains among the stones and old foundation walls dating back to Hellenistic times. I pass the whitewashed chapel topping the hill, with its few small icons and its smell of incense, and sit on a rock below it, out of the wind. The air seems still despite the breeze, and as I gaze out at the pools of sun moving like spotlights on the sea, I have a feeling I've felt on Patmos before: that I'm not only looking at a piece of priceless art but am part of the canvas. By the time I climb back down, my mind is in a childlike state, full of wonder and questions: What were these stones for? Why is the ground terraced and partitioned? What were the people like who lived here? Is this private ground or public? It's a state not only of humility and openness but also of absolute now-ness and delight. And it comes to me more easily and often in solitude.

My final afternoon on the island, I wander without knowing where I'm going, wanting only to be out in the air in the last of the light. A path leads off the asphalt, down a draw, and up again, crossing tiny patches of concrete. To my right I see what seems a perfect scene and feel a strange longing to paint it: the terraced fields separated by walls of brown, gray, and purple stone; the trees within a rocky enclosure; the road that twists its way up a hill, seeming to lead not to something on the other side but to the foundations of heaven. As I follow the path over the hill, I pass a goat with sunshine lighting the side of its head, turning the straw protruding from its mouth into a long, thin shaft of radiance. Beyond him stands a goatherd who returns my smile, his face both brown and red in the radiant light. I wish I could paint him too, but I know the mind's eye carries its images longer.

When I see a strip of green that leads over the spine of another rise, I follow it until a vista opens in front me: rows of red hills running in parallel to streams. This must be what Eden was like, I think, though I can't explain why. The ground is rocky and the brush is small and sparse. But the soil is chocolate brown, the shrubs are fringed in fresh green, and the rocks all look like sculptures rather than random bits of stone. Like Hugo's Patmos,

I think, Eden is a state of mind. I have a feeling, though, that the best is yet to come, and when I clamber up a rocky outcropping I see the sea, its surface undisturbed by anything but gentle waves. There, I sit and watch the hills turn redder still and seem to glow. Above me, the clouds range in color from brilliant white to deep saffron. They billow in one place and then another, skirting a three-quarters moon. I feel as if I'm young and old at the same time, living every happy moment of my life in one glorious instant.

Despite the scene's beauty, however, I want to look at more than just the sun's reflection. So I climb the hill behind me. Suddenly, I'm immersed in dazzling light and everywhere I look—above, below—the world is filled with vivid color. Caught up in the beauty of the moment, I turn and hug the pillar of stone beside me as Stevie Wonder's words float through my mind: *Could a place like this exist, so beautiful?* All I can do is whisper thanks, not only for the beauty but also for the solitude that allows me to experience it so fully and deeply.

The next night, Lax walks me down to the harbor and we pass an old woman in black I've seen before. She has always seemed confused or maybe suffering the pains of age. Whenever I've greeted her, she hasn't returned my greeting. I ask Lax if he knows her and he tells me she's almost a saint. When I ask why, he says she wanders around looking for her son who was drowned at sea, a paragon of love and devotion. Shortly after I board my ferry, I see her spread a blanket on the floor near me, and as she lies upon it, her eyes study me. Perhaps I remind her of her son, I think. I smile at her and pray that God would quiet her heart. I hope she prays for me too.

Later, on the rear deck, as I watch Patmos shrink away, the Chora lights appear to wink at me and I blow them a kiss. There is no question anymore that I'll return...but when?

SEATTLE

The one who walks alone is likely to find himself in places no one has ever been.

Albert Einstein

In the last hour of unseasonable sun, I leave my work in a darkening room to walk the lake. That's what everyone calls it here: *walking the lake*. There's no confusion about which lake you mean because only one lake in north Seattle, Green Lake, is a destination. People drive from miles away to stroll its 2.8-mile path, seeking exercise on a lunch break or relaxing on a weekend.

All I have to do to reach the path is descend a short patch of sidewalk, cross two lanes of intermittent traffic, and navigate a hundred yards of aging asphalt—past a baseball diamond, soccer fields, and a basketball court I've played on since I was young. Because it's only the end of February, there's no one around except the geese that bob on the gentle waves and the rowers in their long sculls preparing for spring races. The sun, so rare this time of year, casts a sheen across the shore, and as I walk I listen to the ducks, the easy lapping of the water, the birds that flit from sunlit tree to dampened ground and back again. This lake has been a part of me since I was small enough to think the wading pool at the north end was a lake itself. In grade school, my friend Nick and I used to paddle across it on inner tubes. In high school, my friend Paul and I would lie beside it in the sun, eyeing girls doing the same thing. For most of the past seven years, I've lived within a block of it, making it easy to walk or run or bike around it anytime I want to. I still meet friends at times to circle it together, but mostly it's become a place of solitude for me—a place I can be alone with thoughts and feelings, day or night.

Early in our lives, we all discover things that become part of who we are. Things that make us happy. Things that bring us meaning. Reading was one of those for me. So was walking. When my mother moved my sister and me from the suburbs into Seattle, we lived in a small house on a safe street three blocks from our church and the Lutheran grade school she must have hoped would help her raise decent children. A surfeit of religion, though, made me weary of the dos and don'ts, the narrow lens through which the church viewed life. When I found alternatives in books, I began to work things out for myself. Lacking anyone to talk to about what I was reading, I started taking nighttime walks with Keena, our toy American Eskimo. Until then, I'd thought of walking only as a way to get somewhere. As far as I knew, no one in my family had ever walked just to walk. Or to think.

It was on those nighttime walks I discovered what, for me, was a kind of magic I could conjure anytime I liked. Away from the seduction of television and the sometimes-suffocating closeness of family in a small house, my mind and heart would come alive in ways I'd never experienced. Suddenly, everything seemed possible, including working through the things that hurt or confused me. Church and school had instilled in me a belief in God, but the God that was there on those walks seemed softer and kinder than the one in sermons and creeds. What I remember most is the joy of feeling I could walk forever without reprimand or interruption or a calling back from where my mind had gone. It was a feeling of being in control of my own life and of being fully and marvelously alive.

I don't know when Green Lake became my place for that kind of walking. That kind of solitude. Probably after college when I returned to Seattle from four years in Eugene, Oregon, where I worked things out by running or biking the lighted paths beside the McKenzie River. I still ran and biked in Seattle, but I found walking better for making sense of what was coursing through me and figuring out who I was or wanted to be.

"In my walks I would fain return to my senses," writes Henry David Thoreau, one of America's earliest proponents of strolling without destination. It's that return, even more than being alone, that makes the type of walking I'm talking about a kind of solitude. Because it's undertaken without intention, even the intention of "getting exercise," it becomes an opening, a mindfulness or presentness that allows our deeper thoughts and feelings to rise—the ones that come to us as little more than intimations in the midst of our busy lives. The beauty of the walking is that it stimulates our bodies just enough to move the blood and make us feel we're doing something other than brooding in a room somewhere. It also changes what's around us, taking us beyond a static place, inside and out. We're in our thoughts, awash in our feelings, but we're moving through a landscape too, able to connect our inner world to the world around us.

While Green Lake has long been my chosen place to walk in solitude, I've walked alone in many parts of the world—Greece, of course, and China. Paris and the Swiss Alps. The Scottish Highlands and the Lake District William Wordsworth made famous. In his poem, "I Wandered Lonely as a Cloud," Wordsworth writes of coming upon a "host" of daffodils and later, in the "bliss of solitude," dancing with them in his "inward eye" as his heart "with pleasure fills." The poem is about two kinds of solitude: the wandering alone that brings him to a thing of beauty and the quiet later that allows him to reflect on it, feeling a joy that lingers past his first encounter.

There is something especially evocative about walking—or running—the lake at night. Wrapped in a cloak of darkness, I feel even more alone. The few others I encounter tend to ignore me entirely, leaving me free to move and think and feel without disruption of any kind. Fidgety one Friday night, I change into running clothes and circle the lake five times. What began as restlessness becomes euphoria as I add lap after lap. And when I slow to just a walk, the euphoria lingers, prolonged by simply moving through this familiar atmosphere without desire or responsibility or intrusion. Sometimes, when I've walked a while, I just sit beside the lake and let my body rest while my mind and heart continue their journey.

Over years, I've walked the lake so many times, my mind and heart become reflective automatically. And my reflections have an element of joy, of positivity, because they happen in a place I love. That bit of joy leavens even the deepest concerns, making it more likely I'll come to a place of peace and harmony than somewhere dark and disturbing. Because of all the pleasure it has given me, the lake has become an atmosphere of love, a place I feel safe enough to explore even the most difficult of interactions or emotions. It combines not only stillness with movement but also familiarity with change. As a result, it fosters finding what I want to cling to while allowing me to let go of what is holding me back.

One of the great beauties of having a lake like Green Lake nearby (or any park large enough to offer a lengthy walk) is that this place of solitude is always accessible. Another is that it offers the chance to be in touch with nature. Lovers of the wilderness might scoff at that statement. In places such as where I live, the Pacific Northwest, there are those who claim that nature can be found—and communed with—only in the wild. A park, they'll say, is an artificial environment masquerading as nature. The good news is: Nature doesn't care what those people say. Nature pokes its tendrils through the concrete crack. Nature sends falcons onto ledges in downtown Manhattan. And nature populates our parks with waterfowl and robins and larks and chickadees and towhees and wrens and squirrels and raccoons and opossums. I've even seen blue herons and eagles perched in trees at Green Lake. What's most important is that being in a place where nature thrives—however limited that thriving may be—creates a context for solitude that is greater than the merely human-made world. It reminds us that we are more than our relationships with other people, helping us to see ourselves as part of something vast and marvelous—especially at night beneath the stars.

Of all the elements that make Green Lake conducive to solitude, the one I might be fondest of is the sound of birds. When I close my eyes one March day, I can discern at least six and maybe seven different calls. Why, I wonder, can't we humans be more like the birds, who seem to sing just because they're alive? They call to one another when they fly together, but just as often they sit on a branch alone, singing for no apparent reason. As I stand there listening, I hear a boy, walking with his father, say, "Shut up, dumb bird." I wonder where he learned to view a bird that way, and why so few of us can still ourselves enough to listen and feel joy. When we're still, we hear and see so many things we don't otherwise. And as we listen and watch, we learn to let them be just what they are. In the process, we learn to let ourselves be who and what we are as well.

SEATTLE

You do not need to leave your room. Remain sitting at your table and listen. Do not even listen. simply wait, be quiet, still and solitary. The world will freely offer itself to you to be unmasked. It has no choice. It will roll in ecstasy at your feet.

Franz Kafka, *The Zürau Aphorisms*

The first thing I do after drinking my morning coffee and recording my thoughts in my journal is clean my apartment. It isn't the kind of place you normally picture when you hear that word. It's actually the upstairs of an old house. A travel agency, with a separate entrance, rents the space below me. The walls in my rooms reach only half my height before they lean in and follow the roofline, which means I can't stand up straight except in the center of the bedroom, the living room, and the kitchen, which is only a corner of the living room. There's a door to a tarpapered roof that serves as a deck and another that leads downstairs to the street. It's really more of an attic space than anything else, the kind of place you picture a struggling writer living, and I love it.

As I enter my thirties, I've added small regional tours of my own (Greece and Turkey, Italy, Scotland, Eastern Europe) to the ones I still lead for Rick Steves. As a result, I travel for five or six months a year and spend much of my time in Seattle planning and selling excursions. My little apartment, where I live alone, is a refuge from the road, but it's also the place I do much of my work, including the creative writing I squeeze in when possible.

As you can imagine, a place this small doesn't take long to clean. And, to be honest, I don't do an entire cleaning very often. But today I'm beginning an experiment, an exercise in solitude, and it seems improving the cleanliness and neatness of my environment will strengthen my resolve to follow through. I won't feel a need to escape the open magazines, unread mail, and dirty dishes pulling me in different directions.

It may sound funny to seek solitude when I live alone, and I'm sure my friends would have a good laugh if I told them what I'm doing. But it's actually harder to find true solitude at home than away. Not only am I surrounded by reminders of my daily work but I have a telephone and an answering machine and a habit of spending part of each day with friends. In other words, either people call me or I call them, and I go out to meet them or invite them over. Even when I'm not in touch with friends, I'm constantly surrounded by the things I leave out on tables and counters and chairs: half-read books, half-finished projects, unanswered letters, unpaid bills. Because I live alone, this messiness, if that's what it is, doesn't disturb anyone. But if I want to pursue the benefits of solitude, I need to put them all away. Give myself a fresh, clean place in which to be alone.

One reason it's harder to seek solitude when you live by yourself is the very fact that you do. You tend to think your daily life is solitary and therefore it's silly to go somewhere else to be alone. But solitude is about more than not having others around, and in our daily environments, even if people aren't physically nearby, they're in our space in other ways. Our minds are full of memories of them, and objects that remind us of them keep them present, including pictures of past events on our walls. Often, those events took place in the very space we're in. It is, in essence, a space of chaos, where past experiences assault us from all directions all the time. Hence the need, as I pursue my experiment, to clean things up. Put things away. Limit the obvious reminders of duties and interactions and former selves.

The internet and cellphones won't be around for a number of years yet, but my frequent interactions with people have made me emotionally dependent on them anyway. I define myself to some degree by my relationships with them. When I'm not with others, I often lose myself in a book or resort to watching television. Except for the time I spend each morning writing in my journal, I don't stop to think about who I am or what I feel or what is most important in my life. Even that half-hour of thought becomes subsumed in the activities of daily living, which thin and eclipse the insights it offers. Rarely do I sustain a focus on one thing. One idea. One emotion.

So I'm trying this experiment: being entirely alone for several days. I haven't told anyone about it, but maybe I should have—at least those who tend to call most often. If I did, though, I know they'd look at me funny. Some would call anyway. Some would take it personally, thinking I just didn't want to be with *them*. And some, who already wonder about me, would take it as evidence I'm unreliable. Capricious. Probably selfish. If they don't know what I'm doing, I figure, they'll leave their messages on the answering machine and think nothing of not hearing from me for a while because I'm often gone anyway.

It isn't until the second day that I actually turn the answering machine off. I think, at first, I can just ignore the messages people leave, but I find that every time I hear one I want to pick up the phone. In fact, I'm so used to picking up the phone, I find myself reaching for it to call someone every time there's a lull in my day. Even in the evening, when I order pizza for dinner, figuring delivery will keep me from interacting with others, my impulse is to call a friend to share it with me. So ingrained are these impulses, I pick up the phone without thinking and have to tell myself to hang it up again.

What I notice first when my experiment begins is how quiet my life is. I live alone in part because I want quiet, but I don't really live in quiet most of the time. I shut the things and people around me out when I sit down to write or read, but even then I'm interruptible. Now, the hours stretch before me and I fear I'll become bored. The truth is, I don't really live alone; I control my space, both the physical space around me and the space between my ears. I'm more like a traffic cop than a hermit. I decide what can enter and what can't. And sometimes I fall asleep on the job or just grow lazy and let everything and everyone in. That's what turning on the television is like. Not only is a bright electronic device that broadcasts anything and everything a huge disruption to whatever I might be thinking or remembering, but a TV projects whatever it has to project, not all of it predictable, even if I choose the show I watch. The same is true of people I talk to on the telephone. I don't know when something someone says will take my mind or heart in a new direction, ending or at least delaying my involvement with whatever was occupying me before the call.

By the end of the third day, my resolve to remain in solitude at home for even a few days has dissolved. My mother calls with anxious concerns about my sister. A friend I haven't talked to in a while asks me to go to lunch. I go out for a walk and run into a woman I know well, who engages me in conversation about the Black church I've been attending. But while it becomes clear to me I need to get away to find real solitude, my attempt to live it at home has yielded some insights. One is that I have more time than I think I do if I will only manage it better. A second, which comes from the first, is that I don't need to push so much. I need only work diligently toward the things I believe in; time will eventually provide both breakthroughs and opportunities. It will bring the right relationships too, if I slow down enough to be discerning.

I'll live alone for four more years before I marry, and in that time I'll develop ways to insure I spend part of each day in solitude, at least when I'm not on the road. Because my apartment is too small to set aside a room or even a table, I'll nurture habits instead that foster calmness of spirit and a sense of being apart. I'll seek my solitude in the early morning, before the day's concerns and events have cluttered it up, and I'll turn off every device that might bother me. Then I'll spend the first few minutes in quiet prayer to center myself. Because a set block of time is, in some ways, the best *place* for solitude, I'll often set an alarm for an early hour, leaving plenty of time to do what I need to do later that day. Knowing I've reserved this time for being quiet will ease my anxiety about getting things done, even on days when I have a lot to do.

Sometimes my solitude is only twenty minutes long.

Sometimes it goes on for hours. After my prayer, it always starts with making an entry in my journal, which calls to mind the things I've been thinking or worrying or dreaming about. Although I record events at times, the main thing I do with my journaling is investigate my state of mind and heart and spirit. I find that if I do this honestly, action often follows. I'll scan my shelves or go to the library to find a book that answers a question. I'll call someone I need to resolve something with. Or I'll sketch out plans for a new project. Out of my solitude have come both new understandings and new directions, as well as a greater awareness of what I value in old friends and old habits.

When I do marry, I'll find that having established this habit of solitude will help me adjust to the very different life of being a husband because my wife, Sylvia, will recognize my need for it and do her best to help me preserve it. When I begin to spend more and more of each day writing, this understanding between us will make it easier for her to let me disappear into the quiet space every writer needs for as long as necessary. I'll try to always keep in mind that her willingness to accept my solitude and limit activities that might disrupt it is a price she pays for it. I hope the dividend she receives in return is a more-present, loving, and self-aware partner, though I doubt she would say that's always the case.

The great beauty in living alone is the flexibility you have to insert solitude into your life without causing disruption to others. But you must *choose* to spend time in solitude rather than assume it is part of your life simply because you live alone. Solitude is an uninterrupted time set apart to reflect on yourself, your life, and your spiritual condition. It opens a portal to understanding and refreshment that doesn't open by itself. At its best, it bleeds into every other minute of your day, making you more mindful and grateful, whether you're with people or not.

Solitude in a Settled Life
(1991-2011)

SAN JUAN ISLANDS

Everything in nature invites us constantly to be what we are.

Gretel Ehrlich

As we follow the other cars onto the ferry, I think back to two months ago when Sylvia first took me to the island off the coast of Washington State where her family has owned property since the sixties. We'd known each other only a month then, and the middle of winter wasn't the best time to visit what was usually a vacation place. But a huge storm had blown through the Northwest and she wanted to see if the two small cabins on the property were okay. Although the ferry that time was just as large as this time, ours was the only car on it. The ferry workers parked us in the middle row by the guard rope at the bow and waves rocked the hull again and again, making us feel as if we were on a massive teeter-totter. When we reached the property—a pie-shaped piece of land with 400 feet of high-bank waterfront—trees had fallen everywhere. Except on the cabins. A water pipe had burst too, and because we couldn't stay very long, Sylvia, who knew how to do all kinds of things I didn't, wanted to return as soon as possible to fix it.

So we're heading back up now. This time, though, I'll be staying when she leaves, hoping a week of solitude in a small cabin at the end of a remote island in winter will clear my mind enough to get some thinking and writing done.

This will be the first of many times I'll seek solitude on this island. When I've married Sylvia and given up tour-guiding for graduate school and becoming a professor, we'll come up for a couple of months each year, with me using the smaller cabin as a writing studio. That modest space—little more than a small main room and a tiny bedroom—will become my place of solitude each summer; a place I can not only write and read but also rest and rediscover myself after another hectic academic year. The island in general will become our place as a couple to escape the city and immerse ourselves in nature—a place of evergreens and ocean spray, eagles and otters, rocky beaches and moonlit nights beside quiet, shimmering seas. Some of my happiest hours will be those I spend at the lower end of the long beach stairs, playing my harmonica or gazing silently across the placid bay, without a boat or human sound to distract me.

The patterns I'll follow on future visits begin this time. When I return to the cabin after driving Sylvia to the ferry, I sit beside a fire looking out at the bay. With nothing of the modern world in my view, I feel a strong connection to all who have occupied this land before, although even the modest cabin I sit in, with its lights and heat and refrigerator, is the height of comfort compared to what they had. As I spend more time in this environment—especially late fall to early spring, when no one else is around—I'll feel an even deeper connection to the non-human world. I'll slow down enough to feel the pace of nature and even, at times, live by its rhythms. I'll see the procession of waterfowl and land birds that migrate through the islands, as well as the mink, newts, and wild turkeys that live here all the time. I'll learn to identify the high pitch of eagle cries, the loud chattering of kingfishers, and the awkward flapping of blue herons in silhouetted flight. With cabins so small and old, I'll spend more time in the open air than I do at home, feeling not only the cold and the wind but the rain and snow.

I'll see spiders, ants, and tiny birds go about their tasks and learn about patience, focus, and perseverance from them. I'll watch, amazed, as misplaced ambition and frustration-fueled anger fall away from my heart. And I'll feel the silence blow through me, sweeping anxiety and clamorous thoughts from my mind. This place where solitude is always at hand will become a place of healing and redirection toward what is good and worth pursuing.

This first time, after hectic days in the city, including arranging tours and reading, with growing dismay, about a war my government is about to unleash, my heart is filled with troubling emotions and I feel scared to write—afraid to confront myself and then the page. Without distractions of any kind, all I really need to do is relax, get sleep, and start my work fresh each morning. But I think of all the wrong things: having a career, making money, what others will think of me if I don't "succeed" in some way. Although I'm here solely to write, in a week I write very little, my output decreased by a malady that will dog me here throughout the years: sinus allergies provoked by the mold and mildew. At times, whether I've taken medication or not, all I want to do is sleep. So I let myself sleep. And I find that the solitude of sleep restores my body and even my mind in ways they need to be restored. The allergies and the sleep slow me down, and I realize what I need most is to learn to slow down—not the pace of my life alone but the rush of my thoughts, the racing of my heart, the turbulent flow of my emotions.

Eventually, I'm able to see beyond myself enough to

appreciate the ways of nature—how, for example, the wind sweeps the leaves and limbs from the trees, dropping them to the earth. How the bugs, molds, and fungi break them down. How the seeds germinate in the duff to generate life. Years from now, when I've secured a tenure-track job in Portland, Sylvia and I will choose to spend my first sabbatical here, living long enough in the woods to be broken down and germinate in new ways ourselves. We'll return to our urban world better able to quiet ourselves and see the workings of nature even there.

One of the most important things I discover during this first island stay is that my plans for a time like this are less important than what the environment does to me and for me, from causing my allergies to flare, to getting me out of my chair to chop wood, to turning my gaze toward eagles that pass at eye level. Despite my fretting about how little I'm getting done, I find a quiet calm and joy growing within me. And when I return to the city—to my relentless tasks and the drumbeat for war—I'll be surprised by how able I am to do the things I have to do in a more measured manner, to stay centered in the swirl of my own and others' needs, and to see with increased clarity and compassion why a troubled and fractured nation wants to rush into battle.

Although I grew up in the Pacific Northwest, where nature is closer at hand than in other parts of the country, my only prolonged exposure to it came when I joined the Boy Scouts and went on fifty-mile hikes along the Pacific Crest Trail or shorter trips into the many forests and wilderness areas near Seattle. During my college summers, though, I worked for the Forest Service on the eastern flanks of Mt. Hood. Although I lived with a firefighting crew rather than in a lookout tower, having trees all around me made it easy to be alone. Spending those formative days in that environment, I came to appreciate what being by myself in a natural setting could do for my thoughts and emotions. College, of course, is a time when you're trying to figure out not only what you will do but also who you are and what's important to you. At school in Eugene, I'd often bike or run by myself at night and spend long hours alone in the library, but others were always somewhere nearby. During those summers, however, I could easily go off in the woods and stay by myself for hours. Even so, I never fully appreciated all that being alone in nature could offer until those later days on Sylvia's family's land.

John Muir once said he went into the woods to lose his mind and find his soul. "Everybody needs beauty as well as bread," he wrote, "places to play in and pray in, where Nature may heal and cheer and give strength to body and soul alike." Being drawn from our minds into beauty, play, and prayer is at the heart of seeking solitude in nature. Some kinds of solitude focus the mind or give it space to reflect on one's life and path. But solitude in nature is as much about watching and listening (and smelling and tasting and touching!) as anything else. When we're still and quiet in nature, we begin to see not only a surface beauty but also a deeper, intrinsic beauty, even when nature is at its most violent and chaotic. Nature encourages us to let something beyond ourselves move us and teach us, to let go of the need to know or do or follow and just exist in a world we were made for. In nature, attention is prayer and movement is play: climbing a rock, crossing a stream, picking up stones or leaves or flowers or feathers. Many times at the cabins, I've done nothing more than sit on the porch or by the sea and observe the changes in the air and elements that are as fascinating as the finest theater. A good play or piece of literature thrills the mind and the heart, but nature, while not ignoring these other parts, renews and invigorates the soul.

In truth, you are never entirely alone in nature, and yet true communion with nature requires encountering it without human companionship. Being alone in the wild connects us to how we came into this world and how we'll leave it, comforting us with the thought that even in our final days we won't be truly alone, whether we sense the presence of God or not.

Nature reminds us that the world of people who can so easily threaten or wound us is only a part of all there is, and can be left behind. It assures us those threats and wounds are not only unnecessary but unimportant. It teaches us by its apparent indifference that we are neither above nor below any other creature, deserving neither of special prestige nor being singled out for abuse. And it shows us in a convincing manner that we are part of a vast whole, vital and dispensable at the same time. There are times when we need to feel our connection to everything and times when we need to know that what we do and say and our mistakes have no real consequences.

Every time I return to Sylvia's family's property, I do so with gratitude, in the knowledge that regular access to the healing properties of unrestrained nature is a privilege many don't have, especially those without resources who live in cities. I feel even more thankful for the opportunity to be alone in nature, which even fewer people experience. Few things could be more sacred or worth pursuing than opening your eyes and ears and heart to the silence and sanctuary of the natural world.

NEW YORK CITY

It wasn't that time stopped in the library. It was as if it were captured, collected here, and in all libraries—and not only my time, my life, but all human time as well.

Susan Orlean, *The Library Book*

On a frigid winter day with snow on the sidewalks and a churned mush of near slush at each corner, I trudge my way up to the university library to find something in the stacks—some book I think I need badly enough to weather the weather, so to speak. I'm in the MFA in Creative Writing program at Columbia University now, and Sylvia and I have been assigned an apartment I think is far better than those my fellow students have received. When the housing application arrived with the offer of admission, I sent it back immediately, assuming apartments would be assigned as the applications came in, and in the notes section I asked for a place "with lots of light." The place we wound up with is at the corner of 112ᵗʰ and Broadway, with the restaurant used for exterior shots in "Seinfeld" across the street. It's only four blocks from the school on an iconic boulevard where it seems something interesting is happening twenty-four hours a day. What makes the apartment truly amazing, though, (besides the $800 rent) is the row of huge windows looking out over Broadway and the low buildings across the street to the Hudson River, the New Jersey riverbank, and the land of the setting sun. *Light!*

But while the light that comes through huge top-story windows makes me feel sorry almost to weeping for those of my colleagues who were assigned lower-floor rooms with only air-shaft views, the apartment doesn't afford us another priority: privacy. It's a one-bedroom, and while Sylvia does her work in the bedroom when she's home, allowing me to write at a desk in the corner of the living room, I need more than just separated space and quiet; I need solitude, if only for a couple of hours. So I head to the one place I've always gone for solitude: the library.

Generally, I read in the large reading room where, at an Ivy League school, the students tend to be respectful of the silence others need to concentrate on their studies. But on this day, the search for my book leads me to an upper floor, where I find a fairly small room with no one in it and nothing around me but books. I'm reminded of the old Christmas lyric: *The weather outside is frightful but inside it's so delightful.* I've lived in New York a year and a half at this point and given up the idea that there's anywhere you can be alone in winter in this urban space with its 8 million people that doesn't require being a multi-millionaire. Yet here's this room that, for now, is a perfect place of solitude.

I can't remember if Samuel Beckett is what I was looking for that day, but Beckett is what I found, a slim novella called *Company*, in which the unnamed narrator is lying on a floor in the dark contemplating aloneness and existence. Perhaps it was the narrator's position that inspired me; after reading the opening pages and wanting to read more, I lay on the floor myself and stayed there, reading and reading and thinking and thinking and never once being disturbed. I read until I'd read the whole book, and when I sat up again I didn't know what time it was or how long I'd been there. I was still alone, still existing in a kind of solitude—free from the noise in a big city, free from the intellectualizing of an Ivy League university, free from the tyranny of my own busyness—and my mind was filled with questions about my own existence. All I knew for sure was that the weather continued to be bleak outside, I was surrounded by books written during the best hours of their authors' days, and I had uninterrupted time to read and contemplate any book I chose.

I developed the habit of going to the library for solitude as a boy. I was a year and a half old when my parents divorced and five when my mother moved my sister and me to a tiny house in Seattle. I don't remember visiting the library from that house, but we must have because I remember coming home with armloads of Dr. Seuss books. A few years later, when I was eight, we moved again, to a slightly bigger house where my sister and I could have our own rooms. Mine was in a basement that was often cold and sometimes flooded. Although I was alone down there, the house could be loud at times and my room was filled with childhood fears and anxieties. Just three blocks up the hill, however, stood the Northeast Branch of the Seattle Public Library, with its window-filled walls and cozy feeling.

The thing I liked most about the Northeast Branch was the quiet. Second most were those huge windows flooding the space with light, an element even more valuable in Seattle in winter than in New York. I can still feel the joy of sitting in one of the small colored chairs in the children's section, tucked into a corner at the front of the building where light came down from two directions. Because the children's section was set off from the rest of the library, no one passed through it who didn't have it as their destination. Many times, I sat alone or nearly alone in that corner, reading the opening chapters of books on the history of rockets or pirates or someone like George Armstrong Custer to decide if I wanted to take them home. When I grew fascinated by model railroads, I spent hours there perusing issues of *Model Railroading*, learning how to turn household items into bushes, buildings, and even people to adorn the areas around my track. What was happening while I was doing these things was the forming of a self, with particular interests and knowledge, curiosity and questions. I lived in a house with few books, where evenings, after homework, were ruled by the television. It was the golden era of children's programming, so I took as much delight as anyone in watching the tube, but my sanctuary, my refuge, my place of solitude was that children's section of the library.

I have no doubt it was the library and the feeling of uninterrupted peace and discovery I found there that made me want to become a writer and, happily, made me suited to that profession. In college, I escaped my raucous dorm, where I lived with a roommate in a space smaller than the average budget hotel room, by going to the library. When I went on an exchange program on the other side of the country and had a roommate who liked to invite his buddies in at the end of the day to smoke pot, I found sanctuary in the library. Even when I returned to Seattle and lived on my own, I would often go to the library to sit for a while, finding in it the kind of "clean, well-lighted space" Hemingway wrote about.

I turned the degree I received from Columbia and a handful of published articles, essays, and stories into a career as a professor. When I ended up in the English department at Portland State University, the office I was assigned was a dark space on a carpet-less hallway. Some of the other professors kept their doors open while they met with students or talked on the phone, and there was plenty of talking and laughter in the hallway as well. My refuge? The library.

Although my focus in grad school was fiction, I became a professor of nonfiction writing, which meant most of the writing I did involved research of some kind, especially the long biography of Robert Lax I worked on for many years. Some of that research involved interviewing, but most of it took place in archives housed in libraries. The two main repositories for Lax's writings and writings related to him are at Columbia University in New York, and St. Bonaventure University in his hometown of Olean, New York, about 350 miles from Manhattan.

At Columbia, the archives were tightly controlled. Researchers worked side-by-side in a small room with the eyes of archives workers always on you. This is a necessary arrangement to prevent theft and damage to documents while making sure papers stay in their proper files and boxes for easy identification and retrieval. In fact, this arrangement is common at most archives. What was different at St. Bonaventure was the trust the archivist showed in me. The Lax papers there (which, for the most part, hadn't been catalogued because of a lack of time and funds) were housed in a small room overlooking the library's main reading room. The archivist would let me in in the morning and leave me to my work. As a result, I did my research in a bubble of solitude, living with the writings I was looking at in a way I couldn't at Columbia. Because I didn't have to ask for each individual file, I could make connections more easily between them and, without others around, think about those connections for hours undisturbed.

This is the greatest thing libraries offer: the ability to access works of intellect, imagination, humor, or history and lose yourself in them without disruption. Libraries foster the formation— and reformation—of a person, a mind, a heart, a soul.

Today, I live a twenty-five-minute walk from the best repository of books in the Pacific Northwest: the University of Washington's Suzzallo Library. Its most distinguishing feature is a reading room built to resemble the great cathedrals of Europe. Its design reflects what has been a lifelong reality for me: the close connection between my development as a spiritual being and my development as a reader and writer. When the teachings of my childhood church began to seem too narrow in a way I was too young to define or articulate, it was the books I found in the library—one leading on to another—that allowed me to see more of the world, hear more perspectives, and, eventually, pinpoint where I felt the religion imposed on me was too restrictive. The library freed God to come to me in a way that felt loving and understandable, clothed in the characters and ideas in those books.

Years ago, I visited a friend who had left Oregon to take a job in Montgomery, Alabama. He wasn't someone who traveled much and he was away from those he loved, as well as the cultural markers he'd navigated by his entire life. He told me as we drove down one of those streets in every city where you see chain stores beside chain stores that he took comfort from seeing them because he knew them from back home. What he expressed is akin to how I view libraries. I know that wherever I am, if I locate a library I'll find a familiar place of solitude, along with containers of knowledge I already know. *Here,* I think as I step inside, *I can be myself without disruption. Here, I know who I am.*

CARBONDALE

The person who writes must always be enveloped by a separation from others...This real, corporeal solitude becomes the inviolable silence of writing.

Marguerite Duras

Sylvia and I have been driving for most of two days, she in our old Nissan Sentra and I in the cheapest rental car we could find. Given how small the Nissan is, renting a second car was the only solution we could come up with to bring all of our things with us. Our route has taken us from New York City, where we've lived for three years, to the edge of the South, where we see the sign we've been waiting for: Carbondale, pop. 25,000. When I received the call offering me a teaching job at Southern Illinois University, we had a hard time finding Carbondale on a map. Now it will be our home. For how long, we don't know. I've been given a contract to teach four classes a term and advise the student magazine. It's renewable for up to five years. But I'm only a "lecturer," being paid peanuts. My main job, as I see it, is to publish as many stories, essays, and articles as I can to secure a tenure-track job elsewhere, preferably closer to our native Northwest.

It's the afternoon before a holiday so we have to hustle to find a storage unit for our things. Once we do, we check into a hotel and begin our search for a place to live. The previous lecturer was single and rented an apartment, but we soon learn that because the town virtually doubles in size during the university's fall and spring terms, apartments are ridiculously overpriced. Having owned property in Seattle, where values are high, houses in Carbondale seem comparatively cheap to us, as is the general cost of living after pricey New York. Our tastes are generally modest, but on our first day of looking for a house, before we've even found an agent, we drive past a place with a for-sale sign that makes our faces light up. It has big white pillars out front, a glass door, a lawn that sweeps up from the street, and, behind a fence we peek over, a swimming pool. We've never owned a pool or wanted a pool and the pool is not the reason we like the house, but it does enhance its appeal. Could we? we wonder. Should we? *Can* we?

We find an agent by simply stopping at the first real estate office we see, and when we tour the house we fall fully in love. It costs maybe a fifth of what a comparable house would cost in Seattle and the monthly payments would actually be less than the rent on a modest apartment. But still, after three years of graduate school, we don't have enough for the down payment. Then Sylvia talks to her mother, who offers to fund the difference, and in a remarkably short time we own the biggest house either of us has ever lived in, on three-fourths of an acre.

Foolish? Gutsy? Privileged? Probably all three. But we're starting a new life in a place we know no one. And I'm going to be doing two jobs, in essence: teaching more than fulltime and establishing myself as a writer. One of the house's greatest assets is it has enough bedrooms to dedicate one to my writing. Even when living alone, I didn't have a room dedicated entirely to the thing I most need solitude for—the room of one's own Virginia Woolf insisted every writer needs. This one runs along the front of the house on the second floor, far from the kitchen and the room beside it where Sylvia will set up her office. In a house with other places I could be alone, there's something different, something special, about having a place where I can shut the door and exist for as long as I want in the solitude every artist needs to do quality work.

I soon discover that having a regular place to be alone is more important than I imagined. Three of the four classes I teach are writing classes, which means constant papers, and the magazine advising requires more time than I expected because no one has ever put together a guide for the students on how to create a magazine. By the time I finish teaching, prepping, and grading each day, I'm too exhausted to even think about writing. Most days, particularly in the August and early September heat, all I have energy for is diving into that blessed pool and floating around. In order to write, I have to get up early and, while my mind is fresh, pour my heart into the thing I care most about before turning to other tasks. Although it means my nights are often short, I set the alarm to give me two hours in what, with the door closed, feels like my sanctuary. It isn't just the quiet, it's also the knowledge that Sylvia respects this space as much as I do and won't interrupt me. Because I'm up so early, no one else will either. The time of day is a place of solitude too.

It's hard to convey to those who aren't writers or artists how important a regular place of solitude is for imagining and creating. Being in a familiar space used only for your art not only eliminates the need for settling in each day, it welcomes you and centers you and cocoons you. It makes you feel as if you're leaving not only the outside world but also your body behind. You can turn off your alertness, the part of your mind that worries about conflicts in the country and climate change, even the part of your heart that loves your family and wants to help those in need. All of these things might become part of what you create, but the tyranny of the immediate, the feeling that you should be doing something in response to them right now, goes away. Like an astronaut entering a capsule, you are free to blast off. Nothing will interfere anymore with the mission ahead.

When Virginia Woolf wrote her book about a woman who wants to write needing a room of her own, she wasn't talking only about having quiet. Before the advent of radio, television, and the internet, homes where educated people lived were often quiet. She was talking about freedom from daily chores, freedom from being expected to give sympathy and comfort to a man whose life and activities were considered more important, and freedom from all of the expectations imposed on women in her day (and still today). What she was talking about more than any of these, though, was respect—for the woman's desires, the woman's chosen work, the woman's right to have an imaginative life of her own. For a writer, a designated place of solitude helps with all of these still. It tells others—and, more importantly, oneself—that the entering into the self writing requires is a valuable, even sacred, act. It says that doing this thing that is out of the norm is important and human, worthy of being encouraged and protected.

In that room, over those three years we lived in Carbondale, I imagined, wrote, revised, and, often enough, published short stories, essays, articles, and parts of a book that earned me a tenure-track position at Portland State University, a three-hour drive from where Sylvia's and my ailing mothers lived. When we looked for a place to rent and then buy in Portland, we made sure it had a space that could be dedicated to my writing. A place of total solitude where creation could take place.

As for that house in Carbondale, after it had served us as a refuge and place of delight in those early years of our marriage, Sylvia, who had picked up a real estate license, was able to sell it herself within two weeks in a market where houses often sat for a year. Having brought thing to Carbondale we'd left in Seattle when we went to New York, we needed more than two cars to carry everything with us this time. So we rented a large truck with a trailer for towing our car. Then, on our way out of town, we stopped by the escrow office to pick up a check for the profit our willingness to be bold in the purchase of a place to live and write and dream had earned us.

WHIDBEY ISLAND

Silence is the sleep that nourishes wisdom.

Francis Bacon

The journey begins with a forty-minute drive from Seattle's Capitol Hill up I-5 to the Mukilteo exit and a twenty-minute motor down the oddly named Mukilteo Speedway before I descend the final hill and ease my Outback to a stop behind the last of the cars parked in the marked-off lane. In summer, when vacationers flock to this island in Puget Sound, the line can stretch up to and over the crest of the hill, and there have been times in winter when I've been able to make it all the way down to the flat parking area at the dock.

But today, as usual, I'm angled downhill several yards from the terminal. The wait is rarely long most of the year because the ferries leave every half hour. In any case, I don't mind the wait because the time I sit on that hill—reading or doing a crossword puzzle or simply contemplating—Is an extension of the solitude I've been steeped in since I left Sylvia's mother's house in Seattle. During the hour it's taken me to reach this point, I've left the radio off and used the drive to let the busyness of my Portland life slough away—the teaching and the theater reviewing, the research and the writing, the conferences with students and even my home life with Sylvia. The two-hour drive to and from my mother's place is the only time I can't busy myself with someone or something else.

I've been a professor at Portland State for four years now, and Sylvia and I have driven up to Seattle roughly one weekend a month throughout that time. We arrive at her mother's house Friday night and the two of them visit or do work together while I leave early on Saturday morning and again on Sunday, if I have the energy, to visit my mother in her nursing home on Whidbey Island. When I first made these drives by myself, I would listen to the radio or maybe a CD to make the time pass quicker. But eventually, as my life became busier and busier, I started leaving the radio and the CD player off, relishing the chance, on a route I'd driven so often I didn't need to think about it, to let my mind rest in the quiet of the car.

After the twenty-minute ferry crossing, I have another forty-five-minute drive to Coupeville, where my mother lives because of its proximity to my sister's house. On the two-lane road across the mostly wooded island, I can feel my body unclenching in the silence and my mind letting go of more and more of the thoughts and worries I've carried from Portland. The solitude of this last stretch is especially important because I want to enter my mother's very different world without bringing too much of my harried one along. With most of my minutes committed to one thing or another at home, it's difficult to gear down enough to sit for several hours in a room where nothing happens except a gentle encounter between my mother and me. Sometimes she falls asleep while I'm there. Sometimes I do, out of accumulated tiredness. Mostly, though, I tell her about the good things in my life and she talks about her pains and memories or my sister's latest activities. Sometimes we just sit quietly. On this day, though, I ask if she'd like to go out in the sunshine, and when she says yes, I put the footpads on her wheelchair and wheel her out.

Because the nursing home is in a rural area, there's a farm-yard next to it, and as we pass it I stop the wheelchair so we can look in at the chickens and horses. I know that for my mother aloneness is not rare. It's a grayness she lives inside, punctured only by the attentions and kindnesses of the nursing home staff, the mumble of her television, visits from my sister and her family, and my calls and monthly appearances. What's rare in her life are movement, open air, the feeling of sunlight on her face.

As I wheel her down the slight slope into the park connected to the facility, I see the empty basketball ring, the never-used exercise stations, and the tall shade trees, but no people. The only sound is the low, wave-like hum from the cars on the island's main road. When we've come here before, we've talked softly and my mother has seemed more relaxed with trees and grass than institutional walls around her. This time, instead of talking, we just sit in a kind of dual solitude, as if we've agreed that this is what we'll do. My mother closes her eyes and lifts her face toward the sun. I lie on one of the exercise benches and close my eyes too. I'm aware as I lie here that she won't be in this world much longer, and it feels like the greatest of privileges—of blessings— to combine being close to her with the solitude I crave. For as long as we stay like this, there are no interruptions or disquieting events, just the sun and the trees and a mother and son who've cared for each other for forty-five years. I wish these minutes would never end, blessed as they are with neither thought nor worry nor conversation but only a deep and silent love.

It is rare to be able to choose silence with another person, and in fact my mother and I don't usually choose it when we're together. We usually invest the too-short times we have in each other's company in sharing and encouraging. But more and more

I've been choosing the temporary solitude that silence affords wherever I can, especially in situations where others choose music or news or podcasts. When I used to jog, I never listened to anything while I ran. I liked not only being alone with my thoughts but also being aware of the world around me, which often drew my attention away from whatever was bothering me. During these short bursts of solitude, the regular rhythm of my footfalls and breathing was my focus, along with the joy moving my body brought me. Today, when I can't run anymore and ride a stationary bike in a windowless room instead, I still prefer to exercise in quiet, sometimes with a book to read.

In those days when my mother was still alive, when I was so busy as a professor and writer and theater reviewer, I learned to steal solitude wherever I could, often by being what many would consider inefficient. Rather than driving, I'd take the bus to work and sit by the window, watching the city go by instead of grading papers or preparing for class. If I drove to school, I'd use the car time to transition between the solitary intensity of my writing and the upbeat energy necessary to animate a classroom. To this day, if I can walk somewhere instead of driving, I will, both for the exercise and for the solitude walking allows me to sink into. For the corporations and tech firms that gobble up many of our best minds, solitude is anathema because it isn't "efficient." To those who think time is money, solitude is a waste of resources, leading to decreased profits. There's nothing in their strategic plans or the inhuman algorithms they call intelligence that says solitude restores, revitalizes, and releases energy.

In his book *Silence in the Age of Noise*, Erling Kagge quotes an email from Jon Fosse in which the poet and Noble laureate tells him: "In a way it is silence that speaks. Perhaps it's because silence goes together with wonder, but it also has a mystery to it, yes, like an ocean, or like an endless snowy expanse. And whoever does not stand in wonder at this majesty fears it. And that is most likely why many are afraid of silence (and why there is music everywhere, *everywhere*)."

Kagge's response to the poet's words reflects the experience of many of us: "I recognize the fear Fosse describes. A vague angst about something I can't quite put my finger on. Something which causes me all too easily to avoid being present in my own life. Instead, I busy myself with this or that, avoiding the silence, living through the new task at hand. I send text messages, put on some music, listen to the radio or allow my thoughts to flit about, rather than holding still and shutting out the world for a single moment."

Shutting the world out for a moment, in order to be present in my own life—that is the gift silence and, on a larger scale, solitude gives me. For the moments I lay in that park with my mother, I was present not only to my life but also to hers and to the life we had shared. There was no fear in me in that moment, but I often feel it when silence descends while I'm with other people, even those I love. Paradoxically, it's the intimacy implied by silence, by a shared solitude, that causes us to fear it and to end it as quickly as we can. Yet that intimacy—with others, with ourselves, and with our God—is what we crave. And when we let it into our lives, we see how much deeper and more profound moments can be when we shut the world out.

A few years after that day we spent together, my mother died, and when everyone else had filed out of the nursing home room she died in—where I had visited her for seven years—I stayed behind and sat alone with her body. Right then, in particular, in what felt like the most significant moment of my life, I wanted both to shut the world out and be fully present. I wanted to feel not only the depth of my loss but also the love and sacrifice and endless care for me that loss represented.

There is no solitude more profound than the one that follows a mother's death. Even when I rejoined my family and Sylvia did her best to comfort me, I lived in that solitude at times for weeks—sometimes by choice, sometimes not. I was fortunate to be on sabbatical at the time, living on an island surrounded by nature, and I often spent hours at a time doing little but watching the movements of spiders and ants and birds as my heart grieved and ever-so-slowly healed.

As Fosse wrote, there was wonder and mystery in that ocean of silent grief, and if I hadn't allowed myself to be present and silent with it, I'd be less fully human now than I am. Less aware of what I don't know and can't control. Less attuned to the wonder of being alive and the gratitude that should go along with it.

"Shutting out the world is not about turning your back on your surroundings," Kagge writes, "but rather the opposite; it is seeing the world a bit more dearly, staying a course and trying to love your life."

KIRKLAND

Fill your paper with the breathings of your heart.

William Wordsworth

Few of us feel more alone than when we've lost someone we love. Solitude in those moments has no redeeming features. It brings an aching that seems unquenchable and a longing for what we can never have again. Grief can make life seem like an endless solitary journey through a dark tunnel with no aid stations along the way. We may love others deeply and appreciate their companionship at other times, but in those moments we feel a sadness that can't be salved, an aloneness that can't be breached, a lostness that leaches the savor and meaning from life.

This is how I feel in the moments after my mother's death. Sitting alone with her body, I feel no desire to be anywhere else— or anywhere at all. I don't want to be alone but I don't want to be with anyone either, anyone but her—and her body, though it grows cold, is the closest thing I have to being with her now. While I sit with it, I can imagine that her spirit is still nearby. But eventually, I stand and force my legs to move, entering what feels like little more than a half-life in which I'll never hear her voice or see her smile or even argue with her, which seems preferable to the silence I'm facing.

Somehow I make it through the evening and the night and, just after eleven o'clock the next morning, sit down in a coffee shop in Kirkland, near the house we lived in when I was born, to start writing about her death. I don't know what to write, so I start with the simplest possible statements: "My mother is dead. She died yesterday at 2:30 p.m." I'm seeking only a way to begin, to start my pen moving, to coax my heart into releasing what it's feeling so my mind can pore over it as it flows through my hand to the page.

Although I'm in a coffee shop and people walk by the window in front of me, I feel entirely alone. Yet putting words on paper makes me feel as if I have a companion who is closer to me than anyone, even God. This companion appears only when I'm alone and when I set down thoughts and feelings in this cheap composition book. I'm not writing a composition now. In a way, I'm not writing at all. I'm doing what I call journaling and others call keeping a diary, but it has little connection to what a journalist does or even a writer. I'm not writing something to read later. Something to revise and make "beautiful." At a moment like this, I'm writing only to survive. To find out what I'm truly thinking.

To dig down and discover my deepest emotions. Although the pain of losing my mother seems inconsolable, I find a measure of consolation in what I'm doing—in the act more than the words or even the emotions they evoke.

I've been processing life in this way for so long, I can't imagine living without it. And yet I've never had to process anything like what I'm processing now. Even so, writing—this simple act—is already making me feel I'll survive. I can live through this morning. And if I can live through this morning, I can live through the afternoon, the evening, the night, tomorrow....

In the days ahead, I'll sit in this same way on the island property Sylvia's family owns. I'll lean over a picnic table on the wooden deck in the morning air and write for an hour, two hours, sometimes three. I'll feel the grief again and again and see it bleed onto the page over and over. From time to time, I'll pause to watch some creature go about its life—a bird rustling through leaves, a woodpecker banging its head against a trunk, an otter swimming backwards through the bay—and when I return to my writing I'll feel a little more alive, a little closer to going about my own life. In time, I'll feel incredibly blessed to be able to do nothing, accomplish nothing, but the processing of grief in this decentered way. I'll realize that by recording what I'm feeling as truthfully as I can—taking the time to sift my emotions as I fashion each letter, each word, each sentence—I'm moving it out of my heart into the world, making it observable in an objective way while, almost coincidentally, leaving a record of it that can be pondered later or, if too painful, put away without ever being considered again. It's the act, not the record, that matters—this way of being alone that helps me make sense of life even when what I face seems nonsensical.

I started keeping a journal for the same reason many others do: I was going on a trip and wanted to record the sights I saw and things I did. I can't remember now if I expected to record my thoughts and feelings as well. I was twenty-four and working as a writer and reporter for an international relief and development magazine. No doubt, I saw my journaling as an adjunct to my note-taking, another way to bring information home. But this was the mid-1980s, when refugees were pouring out of Southeast Asia and the Soviets were in Afghanistan. When I found myself interviewing a young Vietnamese woman who had fled her homeland in a small boat and been raped by Thai pirates or talking to Russian ministers in Kabul after watching rockets flare across the sky that morning, I felt the need to set down more than facts. Soon, I was using my journal to sort out my thoughts on situations of all kinds, political as well as personal, and I never looked back.

As travel became a lifestyle rather than something I did occasionally, my journal was often my only familiar companion. In it, I could carry on the continuous conversation about life that was impossible with a changing cast of fellow travelers. I'd often shorten my sleep in order to have an hour or even half an hour to write before the day began. As my writing shifted more and more from descriptions of places or sights to examinations of my reactions to people or readings or things I learned, I began to see my journaling as a kind of portable solitude. I'd find a coffee shop or a bench by a trail or even a rock beside the sea, and while I sat there lost in what I was writing—what I was thinking and feeling and sometimes dreaming—it didn't matter who or what was around me; I was in a place of my own.

I've been journaling for over forty years now, and it's the first thing I do after coffee each morning. I hardly miss a day anymore. If there's distracting sound around, I slip on a pair of noise-cancelling headphones and enter a cave of quiet contemplation. Some days that means coolly dissecting turbulent events. Other days it means little more than feeling the pleasure of being alive, writing slowly and calmly about whatever brings me joy. Once

I've journaled—once I've spent those minutes in solitude—I feel ready for whatever comes, knowing I'll have that time of private contemplation and self-examination again the next morning. Sylvia has come to understand that journaling is sacrosanct. My journal is my holy of holies, the realm I enter where I meet myself and my God. Whether I write about holy things or not, I'm always aware that I'm in the presence of the divine. And that awareness, along with knowing no one will ever read what I write, frees me to be honest. Compels me to be honest. Makes me ask myself again and again *if* I'm being honest.

Robert Lax told me once that when he was younger he often wrote in his journal as long as he could, making twenty- or thirty-page entries. His intention, he said, was to find out what he cared about. He wanted to see the patterns in his thoughts and writings, the subjects he returned to again and again, the obsessions and viewpoints that recurred most often, as well as the language they were dressed in. By finding these things, he hoped to know himself at a deeper, even unconscious level.

I've never written that much in a single day, but when I read back through my old journals, they're goldmines for the kinds of patterns Lax was looking for. One thing this kind of mining does is help you see what has been stable in your life, which is especially useful when people or events cause you to question yourself or your background or your beliefs. The record I leave in my journal helps me to see I've faced similar situations before and survived them. I'm not reliant on memories alone, which are often distorted by emotions, desires, and the influence of others.

Even if I never look back through my entries, the act of writing every day brings enduring concerns and fears, hopes and dreams, consistently to consciousness. When I feel something unusual, especially a sadness or foreboding, it helps me identify the source and figure out if I should do something about it. If I find myself thinking about the same subject over and over, it helps me work out why. And because I have no agenda while writing, other than finding out what's in my mind and heart, it helps me see patterns I've been living by and discern where they come from—whether they're habits I've developed without conscious thought, ambitions that have skewed my actions, or fears that have made me avoid people or subjects or places.

While journaling is usually a place of solitude, it can be a place of voices too. Sometimes it takes a long time to write myself to where I can be alone. It's when I have reached that point that the real honesty comes. My true self is a shy creature. It can be beautiful and radiant, but just as often it's ugly and dull and has a tendency toward shame. While I like to write about the beautiful, it's writing about the ugly and the shameful that does the most for me. When I write about my shame, it loses its power. This is true of facing those parts of ourselves we like the least anytime we're alone, but sometimes if all we do is sit and contemplate, it feels as if there's nowhere for these negative emotions and evaluations to go. Thinking about them can make them seem bigger than they are. Writing about them externalizes them, objectifies them, preventing them from becoming anything more than themselves. It allows us to offer them more easily to God as well: concrete concerns cemented to concrete desires.

One of the greatest beauties of seeking solitude through journaling is that the act alone can cause a protective bubble to form around you. First, you begin to look for places that are quiet enough for thought. Second, people who might approach you if you're simply by yourself will often stay away if they see you're writing. Third, you learn how to pull into yourself even when surrounded by people or noise. By concentrating your attention on the act of composing sentences and paragraphs, you develop the ability to turn inward and keep your focus there, wherever you are.

It's when I journal that I feel the flow of life most fully: the change and yet consistency from day to day; the possibility of epiphany; the wonder and awe to be found in living, even when nothing eventful seems to happen. Journaling shows me, in fact, that something eventful is always happening, inside or out. I just need to be present to it, in the way I was to my mother and then to her body when she was gone.

COLLEGEVILLE

I feel strongly that the God we meet in solitude is always the God who calls us to community.

Henri Nouwen

I'm weaving playfully up the drive, turning the bike this way and that, the sun through the trees dappling my arms as the summer lingers. I've been here in Minnesota for three weeks and I'm feeling better than I have in months—physically, mentally, emotionally. As a visiting scholar at the Collegeville Institute, I have a two-bedroom apartment to myself, as well as the time I need to work on my biography of Robert Lax *and* learn to play the piano. I thought about walking up to the practice rooms this afternoon, just to enjoy the sun a bit longer, but that would have made me late for the scholars' gathering this evening. As it is, if I play for my usual hour, I'll barely make it back in time. I'm thinking ahead to practicing the techniques my teacher just taught me and remembering riding along like this as a kid...when suddenly something slams my head, turning the day black. Next thing I know, I'm pushing myself up from the asphalt, the hand I lift to my temple dripping blood. My pants are torn and my right knee is stiff and numb. The hand I use to try to stand is a patchwork of cuts and abrasions and feels as if it might be broken. Every part of my body, it seems, throbs with pain. I look over at the borrowed bike, twisted on the pavement, and see the seat lying several inches from its post.

There's no one around and the bike is obviously unrideable, so I nudge it off the drive and start to limp back toward the Institute. It's late on a Friday and I don't know if any of the staff are still around. The drive seems ten times longer than it did when I biked up it and I try not to think about my injuries—what they mean for my stay here—as I limp along. The pain makes thinking difficult anyway. When I come to the end of the trees, I see Elisa Schneider, the business manager, climbing into her car and call out to her, making my voice as light as I can so I won't scare her. The blood from my face is a river now and I'm moving like Frankenstein's monster. When I'm close enough for her to see what I look like, I say, "I'm okay. I'm okay."

Less than a year after becoming a full professor, I've moved to this place in the middle of Minnesota to spend four months mostly alone. I'm one of eight scholars chosen by application and spread across a modest complex of detached dwellings designed by the Bauhaus architect Marcel Breuer. The Institute, linked to St. John's University up the hill, was started almost fifty years ago by Father Killian McDonnell, a Benedictine monk from the abbey that founded the university, with the purpose of promoting scholarship and ecumenical discussion. Its emphasis now is on seeking shared meaning in a natural, spiritual place. I've been here twice before, for week-long writing workshops, but I've never done this kind of extended retreat. Until I arrived, I didn't know if I'd be able to settle myself enough to take full advantage of it. In just three weeks, however, I've done more writing and thinking about my book than over the past half-year at home. Just as important, I've been able to immerse myself in the contemplative atmosphere established by the monks at St. John's Abbey. I've gone on long runs and swims as well, improving my health while pursuing the kind of solitude that lets my mind rest while my body moves.

But now there's this.

The Institute's director, Don Ottenhoff, is still in the main building when Elisa guides me inside and he drives me to the emergency room in the nearby town of St. Cloud. After sitting in a small curtained room for what seems like hours, shivering in a thin gown, I learn that my kneecap has been shattered. A few minutes later, a doctor steers a long needle into the one-inch gap beside my eye, pressing it into the open wound until the pain is so bad I think I'll pass out. When he does it a second time, I know I would never hold up under torture. And this is only the Novocain.

It's already late at night when I hobble out of the hospital on crutches. I have seven stitches half an inch from my eye and a brace on my leg I'll be wearing for the next three months. It isn't until I'm alone in my bed, however, that I feel the full impact of what has happened. The pain when I move keeps me awake and the screws on the brace tear my skin if my legs cross. I don't know that I've ever felt as alone as I do right now, all of my happy plans gone in the snap of a bicycle seat. I came here expecting one kind of solitude and ended up with a different kind: the kind the disabled experience, where being alone is not only isolating but often frightening and even deadly.

I can see before the night is over that what has happened to me will force me to wrestle with the place of others in the pursuit of solitude. My first thought is that I'll have to go home, where Sylvia can care for me. I've come to Minnesota without a car and been dependent on others for rides to the grocery store already. Now I'll have to go to doctor's appointments, and given my need to use crutches, I can't even go up to the abbey to join the monks in prayer without someone's help. It seems impossible for me to stay.

But then, the next morning, one of the staff members, Carla Durand, tells me she'll take me to the doctor and the store, and a scholar I've barely met leaves food outside my door. Before long, Carla has rented a golf cart for me to use, so I can make it up to St. John's on my own for my piano lessons, prayers, and meals in the refectory. Suddenly, it seems the accident might actually enhance my ability to be alone in the way I need to be, helping me keep my butt in my chair and do the work I'm here to do—simply because those around me are caring for me.

The Collegeville model—with scholars and writers working in isolation yet coming together several times a week to share their work and fellowship together—has its roots in the loose associations formed by the first Christian monks, known as the Desert Fathers, in ancient Egypt. In truth, solitude rarely means total isolation from others. Even on Patmos, where I had no regular contact with anyone, I talked to the woman who sold me groceries, had passing exchanges with people on the road, and traded letters with family and friends back home. But until this accident, my experiences of solitude have never included this level of dependence on others.

I remember that Rilke line: "Love consists in this, that two solitudes protect and touch and greet each other." He was talking about a partnership between two people, but I can see now that his words apply to larger groups as well. Without forsaking their own solitude or work, those around me are showing their love by doing even more than Rilke suggests. I think again of the disabled—those in a wheelchair or a bed or forced to stay alone in a room. We tend to assume they're lonely and want our fussing, our control, but how many of them, I wonder now, would prefer humbler assistance that allows them to choose how much solitude they live in?

Knowing I can call on others relieves my anxiety and stocks my cupboards, allowing me to focus on my writing and the contemplation of my busy life at home this time away affords. Because of the accident, I'm more physically alone than I expected, but less alone emotionally and psychologically. With Sylvia calling me regularly and the staff and scholars checking on me, inviting me to events, and helping me in whatever way they can without making me feel they're doing anything special, I feel both alone and attended to by angels. Out of this feeling comes the best work I've done on my book. By the end of my four months in Minnesota, I'll have half of the book finished, with plans for the other half ready.

By the time the brace comes off my leg, I'll be so steeped in the fellowship and Benedictine spirit of hospitality around me, I'll have mostly forgotten the negative spirit at my home university, where suspicion and harmful acts done in secret had worn me out. Yet I won't feel my solitude was ever disturbed.

Although I've come here primarily as a "scholar" and the program I'm in is focused on intellectual pursuits, there's a strong aesthetic component to this solitude too. My apartment's floor-to-ceiling windows look out over a lake where eagles fly and loons sound their haunting calls. One day, when the snows have come, I watch the sun turn a flurry of tiny flakes into little prisms, making it seem as if the world is a shifting kaleidoscope of evanescent rainbows. I've never learned to play an instrument properly, but every day now, thanks to the lessons the Institute has made available, I sit alone in a practice room in a solitude of sound, my hands, as they heal, turning the press of keys into sonic glory.

Everyone should have an opportunity like this, I think, especially those who are caretakers for a family or someone who's ill—a chance to rest, explore themselves, and let their spirit and heart soar.

Shortly after I return home, Don Ottenhoff calls to ask if I'd like to lead a week-long workshop that will replicate my experiences at the Institute on a smaller scale. Called "Apart and Yet a

Part," the workshop will gather writers from across the country for a week of spending their days writing in solitude and their evenings together, sharing meals and fellowship.

One of the first times the workshop is offered, half of the group is women pastors who take off their stoles and their shoes and exult in being cared for as they indulge their passion for writing. During our weeks together, I have the chance to meet with these writers individually and as a group, helping them not only with their writing but also with the structuring of their lives, including finding time to be alone. Again and again, I encourage them to set aside a daily time for writing and reflection, even if it's only fifteen or twenty minutes. Your life will change, I tell them. Your writing too. And the emails they send me later attest to all the ways my words proved true. These periods of solitude not only help them finish their writing projects, as shown by the published books they send my way, but also help them make lifestyle choices, guiding them away from the constant barrage of have-tos most Americans face toward a healthier mix that prioritizes meaning, beauty, and self-care.

It seems fitting that the book my time alone at the Institute helped me write is about a writer and spiritual seeker for whom solitude was the nursery for everything he sought and accomplished. His was a solitude among others too.

"No man is an island/Entire of itself," John Donne wrote. "Every man is a piece of the continent/A part of the main." While it's true that we're all connected, a person can exist as an island at times as well—edging away from the continent while maintaining a connection below the surface. What matters is that we remain in hailing and swimming distance of each other, and that, when the time comes, we help or let ourselves be helped by those nearby. It's important in seeking solitude to remember that being apart is good for a while but we are always a part of something greater: the indivisible human family.

Returning to Patmos
(2024)

God is with those who persevere.

The Quran

I'm making a passionate point in a Zoom call when I first sense something is off. My mouth feels funny. Later, while eating cereal, some of the milk drips through my lips. It isn't until I'm brushing my teeth before bed, however, that I look in the mirror and see that my cheek has slumped, like a hillside heavy with rain. I spread my mouth in a smile but only the left side rises. With fear growing in my heart, I raise my arms and say a few words to see if my speech is slurred. Then I stand on one leg after the other to check my balance and take a few steps to see if my foot drags. Finally, I call Sylvia into the bathroom to see what she thinks.

The trip I've had planned for months—a return to Patmos at the same time of year I first went there thirty-nine years ago—is only six days away. I've made arrangements to spend two weeks alone in Robert Lax's old house to see how different total solitude might be as an older man. I'm sixty-five, an age when anything might go wrong, but I've never bought travel insurance. Until now, my health has been fine.

When Sylvia sees my smile, her first thought is the same as mine: stroke. "But I don't have any other signs," I say. And when I look my single symptom up online, another possibility appears—Bell's palsy, a sudden slumping and numbing of the face on one side. My cheek is slightly numb, but otherwise I feel okay. So I decide to wait until morning, to see if my condition has changed, before doing anything.

When the slumping is still there the next day, I call my doctor's office and get an emergency appointment with a different doctor, who does a few physical tests before sitting me down and saying, "This could be Bell's palsy, but I think you've had a stroke." Then she sends me to the emergency room.

As Sylvia drives me to the hospital, I look out the window at the drab day and think: *This is it.* Everyone who lives to my age knows that a day will come when your life will change. Something will happen, your health will falter, and you'll realize you're old. If I've had a stroke, I think, I can't go on my trip and I might not travel again. I wonder suddenly how many years I have left.

The emergency room is full and the triage nurse doesn't consider my condition dire, so we settle in for a long wait. When my name is finally called, I'm directed to a bed in a hallway and a young doctor appears. After replicating some of the other doctor's assessments and adding more, he orders a battery of tests: bloodwork, an EKG, an MRI, and a CAT scan. I lose track of the hours as I'm poked and hooked up and slid into noisy machines. Back on the hallway bed, I open the medical system's portal on my phone and wait for results. Those for the bloodwork come first. They're all normal. The EKG shows a slight irregularity but otherwise it's normal too. The last to arrive are the most important: those for the scans. As I scroll past terms I don't understand, I see one word again and again: normal. When the doctor appears, he prescribes two pills for what he's fairly sure is Bell's palsy and an ointment for my eye because the condition keeps your eyelid from blinking or closing all the way. When I ask if it's okay to go to Patmos in five days, he says, "I don't see why not."

His answer is the one I want but it doesn't keep me from feeling anxious as I travel for thirteen hours from Seattle to Greece. Illness, even when treated, has a way of turning solitude into loneliness and fear. As I wander the streets of Athens alone on my birthday, my joy at being back in Greece is tempered by melancholy. I wonder if I've made a mistake. If I've let myself believe I'm still the young man who traveled so blithely and worry-free. Before long, though, I'm riding a modern subway to the port of Piraeus, looking down at my pack as I did on the bus the first time, and feeling the joy of heading to the islands. This time, instead of a portable typewriter, I'm carrying a comforter friends in Athens have given me in case Lax's house is too cold. And when I reach the port, instead of having to scan wooden boards, I find a digital sign on the side of a ferry that lists "Patmos" among its destinations.

Seeking to replicate my first visit, I'm not only carrying a backpack (after using a roller bag for years) but have purchased the cheapest ferry ticket possible, which doesn't give me access to any salon or room. I have the old *Ialyssos* in my mind, but the ferry I board is more like a cruise ship. An escalator whisks me up to the reception floor and I can't even find a rear deck to perch myself on as I did the first time. Instead, I choose a padded chair in a corner and, when the ferry has left the port, enter a nicer room with recliner seats. Because it's winter, perhaps, and the ferry is fairly empty, no one seems to care. It feels like cheating to ride to Patmos in a comfortable chair in a warm room without noise or smoke. But solitude is my goal, not deprivation or nostalgia, so I settle back to read and doze and the eight-hour trip passes quickly.

It isn't until I walk out onto the wet side deck with less than an hour to go, hoping to see the lights of Chora, that I notice a set of steps toward the stern. At the top of them, I find a large, covered outdoor area and, behind it, a small rear deck. There's no one on it and a full moon is shining down through a clear sky. When I walk to the railing and gaze at the waves, the water churned white by the ferry's propellers, it starts to feel like old times. Maybe because I've finally had enough sleep or because the drugs prescribed for my illness are out of my system, I feel physically good. In fact, I feel young. For a moment, it seems I could be twenty-seven again, traveling to an unknown island for the first time.

It isn't until I return to the side deck, however, and see, in the distance, what look like tiny lights, that I feel my heart really stir. The lights grow steadily larger until I know without a doubt they're the lights of Chora. They're fainter and smaller than I remember, but soon I can make out the dark form of the island below them, and then the boat is rounding the headland and the sea-level lights of Skala are straight ahead. I scramble below to watch from the car deck as the loading ramp clangs into place. When a crewman gives the okay, I step out into the 2 a.m. darkness of Patmos—alone, for the first time in eighteen years, on this island I once loved so much.

Because of the ferry's arrival time, I've booked a room for the first night. Having learned that the Rex is closed for good, I chose the Villa Zacharo, which turns out to be the place I saw men watching movies when I walked at night my first time on the island. My room at the Villa looks so much like those at the Rex, it seems again that I could be twenty-seven, experiencing real solitude for the first time. Although it's the middle of the night, I'm too amped up to go to sleep right away, so I take out one of the few books I've brought with me: Victor Frankl's *Man's Search for Meaning*, which I read my first time on Patmos. It's about Frankl's experiences in Auschwitz and how they led him to found a branch of psychology called *logotherapy*. In his preface, Harvard psychologist Gordon W. Allport writes that living in a concentration camp stripped Frankl down to "naked existence" and quotes

Frankl on the only freedom this condition left him with: the ability to "choose one's attitude in a given set of circumstances."

Old age is not the same as being tortured and worked to death in a concentration camp. Or losing your family to mass execution, as Frankl did. But there is a sense, as you age, that you are being stripped down. That the things that gave your life meaning are being taken away one by one. When I was young, for example, I was strong and able to do anything. Now, I worry about my heart, and on this trip I've dealt with the side effects of medications. On top of that, I'm no longer the energetic young man people seemed to instinctively like. As an older man, I'm often invisible. My desire for meaning hasn't changed, however, and that's what Frankl's book is about. Allport mentions that Frankl was fond of quoting Nietzsche: "He who has a *why* to live can deal with any *how*." The quote is particularly apt for the old. As we age and the losses pile up, we find ourselves more in need of a *why* to live than ever before.

In my case, Frankl's writings are calling me out of the comfort of my current life and back to the simplicity and passion for meaning that characterized the younger me. This trip and the book I'm writing are all about meaning: the search for it, the need for it, and its elusiveness. When I turn off the light to go to sleep, I think about my desire when young to find the one thing I should do—the one thing that would give my life meaning. What would I say now, I wonder, if someone asked if I'd found it? The answer, I realize, is that meaning hasn't come to me in one lump sum but rather from a variety of sources: a connection with God, love of learning, writing, teaching, a loving marriage, relationships with family and friends old and new, concern for the poor, engagement with issues, desire to make a difference, an ability to feel deeply, a willingness to spend time with anyone I meet, a pursuit of health, cross-cultural experiences, literature, history, science, art, travel, photography, journaling, nature, kindness, simplicity, beauty, and a habit of sitting still and gazing at the world in awe. The search for only one source of meaning, I realize, can blind us to the fact that meaning is all around us and inside us, often in the smallest, simplest things.

Solitude doesn't give me meaning so much as help me see where my life has meaning and where it doesn't. It gives me the stillness and impetus I need to face myself and the life I've lived. The life I'm living. It helps me discern what is true for me without the undue influence of others and what is preventing me from experiencing even deeper meaning.

What voice can equal the voices of solitude? What sights equal the movement of a single day's tide of light across the floor boards of one room? What drama be as continuously absorbing as the interior one?

Jessamyn Ward, *To See the Dream*

I wake up the next morning to glorious sunshine and walk past whitewashed buildings I once knew well to the plaza at the center of Skala. Although I've been told Patmos has changed—and I notice the yoga studio, fashion boutique, and health food store that suggest affluent tourists—most of what I see looks no different than it did decades ago. From the plaza, I pass up a narrow lane, past the stationery store where Lax bought his paper, and soon I'm like an aging salmon swimming instinctively to its spawning grounds. When I reach the top of the hill and see the familiar blue door, the rapid beat of my heart isn't all from climbing the steep stairs. Suddenly, the past is present. I know Lax won't be waiting behind the door but it feels as if he might be.

Inside, however, the house isn't the same. The bed is still in the main room but it's different from the one Lax had there. The table I sat at when I visited him is gone, as are the tables along the walls where he kept his writings, pens, and art supplies. The pictures, postcards, and children's drawings have been stripped from the walls. And everything has been scrubbed and painted. The only real reminders of Lax are the bookshelves filled with his books and his face on a poster above one of his better-known poems:

turn
ing
the
jun
gle

in
to
a
gar
den

with
out
des
troy
ing

a
sin
gle
flow
er

I don't feel sad the house has changed. In fact, I'm glad. I didn't come here to live in a museum. If I want access to Lax's mind and spirit, they're there in his books: those he published and those he read or received from friends. I'll certainly think about Lax while I'm here—his life alone in this small room with its single window—but I've come to concentrate on my own life. My own solitude. With his example as inspiration.

Here are my rules for this time alone: no internet; no cellphone use except to check the weather and send emojis to Sylvia each morning to let her know I'm alive (and receive hers in return, letting me know *she's* alive); no use of my iPad other than for reading downloaded books; no conversations with anyone that aren't absolutely necessary.

There's a small space heater in the house, but I know electricity is expensive on the island, so I buy a blanket at the store to add to the comforter. I buy enough food to stock the tiny refrigerator and cupboard too. After that, I have no need to go anywhere or interact with anyone. Now, I ask myself, what am I going to do? All I want to do after carrying heavy bags up the stairs is relax. "Well, do that then," my mind says. "You're here not to work but to be alone and quiet and alive to the moment."

I can see immediately that I needed this: to be pulled away from the screens, electronic devices, and interconnectedness through the internet that have filled more and more of my time. As I scan Lax's shelves, with their books on philosophy and religions, I think about what he filled his mind with and what I've put into mine. I think about his slow and careful movements too. When I was younger, they seemed the movements of an old man; now I can see the advantage to moving slowly whatever age you are. As I let myself sit instead of jumping up to do something, I feel my relationship to time shifting already. Instead of a vessel to fill, it seems a space to exist in—a space where I might find the centeredness and freedom I'm seeking.

Eventually, I decide to go for a walk before the sun sets. Walking was always my favorite thing to do on the island. As I stroll a secondary street I once knew well, I notice again what little has changed—the houses, hotels, clotheslines. Just as I reach the plaza in Skala, it begins to rain and I hurry back up the hill. A pinkish light spreads through the clouds, and from Lax's porch I see a rainbow arching over the harbor below me. From where I stand, it looks like a protective dome with a pinkish tint inside it. This can't be real, I think, but then I remind myself that Patmos is where the line between dreams and reality blurs.

I was not looking for my dreams to interpret my life, but rather for my life to interpret my dreams.

Susan Sontag, *The Benefactor*

That first night in Lax's house, actual dreams fill the fitful sleep of a jetlagged man beginning to shift to living simply in solitude again. When we remove the things that occupy our daily thoughts and cause the fluctuations in our moods, it leaves a void in our minds and hearts that fills with what has been kept below the surface. During all of our busyness we acquire layers and layers of unexamined impressions, feelings, and anxieties. If we don't stop from time to time to consider them—to clear them out—they pile up. Then, if we ever do stop, as soon as we remove the outer layer, the next one appears. And the next. And the next. One of the hardest and most valuable parts of spending extended time in solitude is how it allows these layers to surface and be addressed.

The first thing I'm faced with, made clear by those dreams, is the disconnect between how I've been living in recent years and the simplicity I lived in as a younger man—the kind of simplicity I've returned to in Lax's house. The first dream is filled with sexual images like those I absorb night after night from the movies and TV shows I let myself watch. In the second, I worry that thieves are targeting my nice home. The third is focused on computer videos, a reminder of how much time I spend looking at a laptop screen. And in the fourth I tell my wife I want to buy a boat. I don't really want to buy a boat—in fact, I'm not much of a buyer of things at all—but as an American I'm exposed every day to advertising, and advertising is all about buying things. Taken together, these images reflect the privileged life I live, the milieu I live in, and the things that distract me from what's important.

What I realize when I wake up is that living the way I'm living on Patmos—a way of life much closer to how I lived when I was young and how Lax lived in his later days—makes it easier to sympathize with the plight of the poor or Frankl's concentration camp victims. Living in Lax's humble house, for example, I feel the cold. Even the water is cold, except for the small amount I heat to dribble over my head when I shower. The food I eat is simple food. And everywhere I go, I walk. Living the way I do at home, immersed in convenience, it's harder to imagine my way into the lives of those who have little, even though I have memories of living much closer to the ground myself. I used to lament lacking money as a child and as a young adult, but now that I have more than I need, that lack looks like its own kind of privilege.

My dreams end with an interesting coda: just before I awake, I hear a sweet, soft female voice say, "The end." The words come to me in the color of lilac, as if to signal that the first of the tests I'll endure during this time alone has ended.

Over the days ahead, more uncomfortable dreams will appear but none as disturbing as those first few. The thing that will test me more is the coming to mind of times in my life when I've been at odds with others. Freed from all that occupies me at home, it's harder to avoid examining my own actions and words in past situations that troubled me. I could lose myself in books, of course, or refuse to let the harder things stay in my mind, but I let them come, one by one, and do my best to review them fairly, including assessing what I contributed and why. It's hard to look at the ways I added fuel to the flame even when I didn't start the fire, and how my assumptions, reactions, and ambitions caused me to hurt others without intending to. It's almost equally hard to accept that others sometimes hurt me intentionally or, instead of viewing me as a human being, saw me only as an obstacle to a goal.

By doing this kind of examining, I'm digging down through layers of accumulated anxiety like a man digging a well, hoping for life-giving water. The key, it seems, is to look at all of these situations with clear eyes—to let them be just what they were, without judgment. If I can do that, I can lessen their effect on my life and find forgiveness for those who seemed to want to hurt me. They were acting out of their own fears, ambitions, and neediness, I know, and I often grew as a person from facing their adversity. In addition, even the darkest days offered compensatory blessings—a time of play with an innocent child, for example, or a faithful friend who listened when I needed to talk.

This kind of review is an important part of solitude—a part that is harder when you're older because you've done so much more living. You have to let everything pass like a long parade of people and experiences to bless, one by one, as they reach you. As I review my own parade, the darkness that has shrouded some of my memories begins to lighten, and I find myself forgiving the younger me as well as those who treated me poorly.

Many people do similar work in therapy, with a professional to help them dig and make them feel safe as they do so. The difference for me is that digging is not my goal. All I've come to Patmos to do is exist in prolonged solitude. No one's agenda is guiding me, not even my own. I'm simply opening myself to myself—and to God. What happens then is undetermined. My only counselors, if you will, are the books I read, which I turn to less for help than exposure to a wider variety of views and ways of understanding life. I learned long ago to bring my whole self to books, to view them as sources of wisdom even if they aren't wisdom books. At the least, if I don't restrict myself to books that reinforce what I already know or think, they take me out of myself and my world, beyond my way of seeing things.

One of the books I've brought along is a history of solitude that features a study by an eighteenth-century writer named Johann Georg Zimmerman. According to the history's British author, David Vincent, Zimmerman gave two criteria to use in deciding whether solitude is "healthy": 1. Your reason for choosing it. 2. Whether or not you return to society after it. An intention like mine—to examine my life alone with God—passes Zimmerman's test, as long as I don't linger too long. Vincent goes on to say that British "gentlemen," in the century after Zimmerman, thought all solitude was aberrant. Life could be lived only in society, they said, where the manly virtues could be displayed. To their minds, those who chose solitude were weak shirkers of their social responsibilities. I would counter that today it takes not only courage but fortitude to choose to be alone to contemplate your life and the norms of your community and world.

Every day I'm here I feel my need for this time more deeply. A time to restore my perspective and empathy. A time to let my lifestyle and thinking be challenged. A time—and place—where awareness of the elements and my own vulnerability can restore my sense of what it means to be human.

When I ask myself how I'm different from the younger man who came here long ago, the answer surprises me. Other than having an older body and suffering from fewer emotional extremes, the only difference I see is that I'm more fearful. And the thing I'm most fearful about is my heart.

I think these difficult times have helped me to understand better than before how infinitely rich and beautiful life is in every way and that so many things that one goes around worrying about are of no importance whatsoever.

Isak Dinesen, *Out of Africa*

I almost didn't include what I'm going to tell you next. My health is a private thing. But I told myself I'd tell the full story. Reveal what it's like, as an older man, to spend two weeks in extreme solitude. For a number of years, I've been susceptible to what is called atrial fibrillation (a-fib for short), an ailment in which the heart can flip into arrhythmia, increasing your risk of stroke. A-fib presents in me mostly as a thumping in my chest and an irregular pulse. I have what's called paroxysmal a-fib, which means it happens only occasionally. The onset usually comes after adrenaline-fueled exertion, sudden emotion, or certain medications. The combination of prednisone and the anti-viral I was prescribed for my Bell's palsy brought me close at times, but I made it to the island and through the first day without incident. Then, as I was climbing the steep hill to the house on the second morning, carrying heavy groceries, including a brace of six liter-size bottles of water, I felt something shift. When I put a finger to my neck to check my pulse, it was racing and then dancing. Not a waltz or even a swing but a two-step here and a jitterbug there. An a-fib episode had begun.

It's hard to describe what it's like to lie on an island 6,000 miles from home, with no one you know nearby and no good medical facility, holding a finger to your neck as your heartbeat varies wildly. It seems your world could disappear in an instant; your heart give out and leave you there, cold and lifeless. On the morning of my second day, just before the a-fib began, I was thinking that I could let go of my fear. After all, my heart had survived taking and going off drugs, crossing so many time zones day had become night, eating and drinking irregularly, sitting for long hours without exercise, and carrying heavy weights up a steep hill. It seemed I could easily slip back into the lifestyle I'd once lived on Patmos: writing and reading and wandering at will, including scrambling up hillsides. Now, it seems I've made a terrible mistake.

As I lie with my heart in disarray, afraid to do anything but read and nap, the insidious thought I have to fight is that I should be *working*. This is a sign, I think, that I need to loosen my grip on my mind, my heart, and my habits. I often wonder at home if what I do on any particular day matters. Lying like this, the answer is clearly no. What matters is only that I try to make every moment as meaningful as possible, whatever the circumstances, even if that means merely lying still. Live this moment, I tell myself. This illness. This now.

When evening comes and I turn out the light, I lie in the dark, listening to the violent wind outside without worrying when or if I'll fall asleep. My heart has settled into a gentle though still-irregular pattern and I try to focus on being aware of being here, being warm, trusting that God is with me. Strangely, despite the turmoil in my heart, I feel at peace. I'm alive in this moment, I think, and that's all that matters. In truth, it's restful to lie like this: a sentient being in a quiet world without distractions or pressures or need to do anything at all. I'm aware as I lie here that every moment in this place is a gift I probably won't experience again. I doubt I'll ever repeat what I'm doing. I may not even return to Patmos. And yet I'm here now, on this island and in this house that have meant so much to me.

I'm disclosing this episode in part because it increased my sense of being alone to the point where I could imagine death, when every one of us will feel alone. I'm disclosing it also because, unsettling as it was, it actually lessened my fear. The worst I'd imagined had happened, and although it lasted fourteen hours, I came through it okay. Afterwards, I was wary and careful—climbing the hill more slowly, step-by-step, and checking my pulse as I walked—but I felt freer and more realistic too. It was so very clear at that point that I wasn't in my twenties and solitude could never be the same as it once was. Instead of an echo from a distant past, it insisted on being its own adventure.

Later on the morning the a-fib ends, I take the first of what I hope will be many walks to places I once loved. My destination is Grikou, with its monks' rock. Although it's January, the sun is out and the air is so warm I strip down to my T-shirt. The walk leads me along the sea, where the ocher cliffs plunge into sapphire water, and I move slowly at first, not only to take in the view but also to guard my heart. Despite my concern, it beats normally, even when I climb the hill that gives the first view of the whitewashed village. When I come to the rock where the monks lived, I move around to the water side and find the cave where I once played my harmonica. It's surprisingly clean and empty. Gazing across at the smaller island I once wrote a story about, I have the same feeling I had all those years ago: of being alone in the world—alone in a place people chose to be alone 1,700 years before me. I have no harmonica this time, just as I have no novel or other project for my days on Patmos. I'm just here. And the cave is just here. And the sea and the smaller island and the sun. My heart is beating the way a heart should beat and my soul is resting the way a soul should rest.

When you take a flower in your hand and really look at it, it's your world for a moment. I want to give that world to someone else.

Georgia O'Keeffe

It would be reasonable to ask how you fill twenty-four hours a day, day after day, without someone to talk to or a project to work on and no real sights to see. I might have asked myself the same thing before I saw how easily hours fill with a combination of necessary tasks (washing dishes and clothes by hand, for example), journaling, reading, walking, and simply sitting in one place or another. Except for short meditations and a daily session of focused prayer, I don't pursue religious practices or other borrowed activities. Freed from interactions with others, as well as their scrutiny, I walk around like Tevye in *Fiddler on the Roof*, talking openly (though rarely out loud) with God.

What's unusual about our relationship, perhaps, is that I don't feel, as many religious or simply spiritual people do, that God is engineering what happens to me or what I might learn. It seems my God is more interested in quiet relationship than being the architect of my daily life. Take my dreams, for example. I don't believe God is directing and producing them to teach me something. I believe they arise from the deeper recesses of my psyche and heart and God is there when I wake from them to assist in my discernment about them. This kind of relationship helps me to sense more clearly what I should or shouldn't do, not to gain favor or avoid punishment but to learn to live in harmony with all life.

Instead of the coffee I have at home, I've chosen to drink only tea, consuming it with slices of bread fresh from the bakery, slathered with raspberry jam. As the tea water warms, I gaze at the sunrise out the window, and if it's especially lovely I take my camera onto the porch. Unlike at home, where everything is quick and easy, I have only a hotplate to cook on and it's slow to heat up, so I'm able to savor these moments. I savor the time it takes me to prepare my lunch and dinner too, telling myself to be present with what I'm about to put in my mouth. When I eat, I focus on each bite, savoring the flavor. As a result, the food, though it's simple fare, tastes as good as any I've ever had. It helps that the vegetables and fruit are mostly locally grown rather than having been picked too early and shipped from far away.

Giving anything your full attention takes longer than not doing so. After my breakfast, I open my laptop to journal, and most days I write for two or three hours. I rarely write that long at home, but slowing down and paying attention means seeing more than you saw before, and having more to say about it. Too often at home, I simply record what I've done and a couple of hasty thoughts. Here, I move slowly enough to make connections between what I see or do and other parts of my experience: not only thoughts or feelings but things I've read, impressions I've had, and memories that arise in the midst of quiet contemplation.

It seems at times that everything here is connected, not just to me or my own past but to everything else. The markings on a rock I lift from the beach, for example, remind me of fossils, patterns in drapery, and the power of unseen forces to shape the environment around us. My experiences here are so small they can seem insignificant, yet the attention I give them makes the supposedly larger things I fret about at home feel less important than the humblest pebble or flower or lap of a wave.

The key is being present. Fully present. Even while pondering the past. Now, as Lao Tzu once said, is the was of what will be. Focus on what is in front of you and inside you, I tell myself. Start with breathing and heartbeat. Start with what you see and feel. Start with awareness of who is in your world. Who is connected to you. Love the breath and the pulse, the sights and the feelings, the ones you know well and those who only pass through your life. Despite the occasional loneliness, focus on what a gift it is to sit here without distraction, immersed in love. Some might scoff at the thought that love is all around you on an island 6,000 miles from home. But it is. It showers down from above, rises from the earth, and emanates out of you. All you have to do is acknowledge it.

Late one afternoon at the end of my first week on the island,

I finally trust my heart enough to brave the climb up the long hill to the town of Chora. I take the old road, with its pavement of rough stones, until I reach the Cave of the Apocalypse, where St. John had his visions, then follow the paved road the rest of the way. The hill shelters me from the wind and the late-day sun glazes the land in a soft, almost-buttery yellow, giving the green that is everywhere this time of year a radiant glow.

I feel seduced again by this land, and it isn't just my old love bubbling up. It's something new as well, some feeling that seems possible only because I'm older. Maybe it's only the sense that the time I have left in this world to feel and appreciate this beauty is limited. When I reach the top, where the monastery stands, the views are breathtaking. Islands rise up out of the sea through limpid air. Fields stretch between rocky hillsides, greener than suburban lawns. Waves wash against ocher cliffs with whitened intensity. Alone in the stillness, I drink it in, watching the lights of Skala come on. After a week in solitude and silence, I see that the spiritual part of this journey is every part.

Standing alone at the top of the island, I feel more fully than I have before that God is with me, not in some spectacular way but in the most ordinary way possible. I sense the divine in the air I move through that moves through me. I am in God and one with God but also companionable with God. And this experience is quiet, ordinary, and ongoing, even at home. The only difference here is I'm alone enough, still enough, and settled enough to be aware of it. Unlike my first time on Patmos, here is not really different from home, except that the things that are layered over my life at home have been stripped away. There are no epiphanies this time. No revelations. Only an ongoing sense of presence in all I think, feel, and remember.

Over my last week on the island, I spend more time outside, walking to everywhere I once knew. One day I walk all the way to the far north beach of Lampi, where I pick up a beautiful sea-polished stone to take to Sylvia. On my way back to Lax's place, when I come to the high hill I have to climb near Kampos, I see the sun near the horizon and feel a weariness from all of my walking. It will be dark when I get back, I think. If only someone would give me a ride. This thought has hardly been thought when I look up and see that a car has stopped beside me. The driver is tan and maybe fifty, with the thick body of someone who works with his hands. Rolling the window down, he asks, "You going to Skala?" When I tell him yes, he nods me over to the passenger side.

After so many days alone, it feels odd to be so close to a stranger, but the goodwill of Patmians like this man—and those who did similar things years ago—makes me feel everyone here is a relative. As we roll along through the evening light, he tells me his name is Avro and asks if I'm visiting relatives or friends. For some reason I mention Lax, who's been dead for twenty-four years, and he says immediately, "I remember him. Tall?" When I nod, he says, "He was a friend of mine. When I was a boy." Connectedness everywhere.

The walks I remember most fondly from my first time on Patmos are those I took at night. I haven't gone out in the evening at all this visit, so one day after dark I take my flashlight and walk to the old monastery road, where I lay on a stone wall decades ago and gazed at the stars. There's no one around when I arrive but I hear the sounds of voices and motorbikes, cats and goats through the clear air.

I remember the stars shining more brightly here than at home, the Milky Way so brilliant it seemed to cast a shadow. But sadly, Patmos has become like much of the world: polluted by human-made light. Although the night is cloudless and moonless, I can hardly make out the Milky Way. The stars I can see seem fixed on a flat surface rather than floating at different depths as they did when the night was darker, the starlight more vivid.

This feeling that Patmos has changed too much becomes

more pronounced as I walk home. When I used to walk with Buby at night, we rarely encountered a car or even another person. Now, as I walk the same road, past the eucalyptus trees and the basketball court, the cars, with their lights, come at me one after another. How diminished my experience would have been, I think, if things had been like this back then.

It was in the dark of those old walks I thought about who I was and wanted to be. Although I'm closer now to the end of my life than the beginning, this time has been filled with similar musings. The difference now is I have more evidence from which to determine who I am and less time to become the person I want to be. At first, the evidence made me critical rather than proud. As I remembered difficult times, I hated that I had caused anyone to ever be angry or sad, and I could see I'd done this often. Over time, however, my view evened out. I began to see that I had done much good and made many people happy too—inspiring them, caring for them, helping them find joy. I'm more able now to focus on my strengths without losing the humility awareness of my failings provides. All I have done and experienced, I realize, has worked together to make me who I am, and I can't give my best to the world if I second-guess myself because I failed at times to live by a higher standard. The only way to give my best is to evaluate my life honestly and take every opportunity to love.

Joy is like restless day; but peace divine
Like quiet night.

Adelaide Ann Procter, *Per Pacem ad Lucem*

I am an advocate for joy. Joy is what I pray for every day for myself and others. But joy isn't the goal of seeking solitude or moving closer to God. The goal is to know ourselves better and fill ourselves with love so we can spread the spirit of love throughout the world. For me, this means learning to be more fully alive and more caring toward those in need or sorrow.

I have one other goal as well: to observe and bear witness to reality as I see it—in essence, to God as God is manifest in the world. To do this, I have to slow down, just as I have to slow down to love. I've realized during this time alone that I, like so many others, have been pushing and pushing, one way or another, for far too long. There has always been a reason to push and then to push harder. Now, I'm learning again what I learned from Lax years ago: to be fully alive and fully loving you have to move slowly. You have to have patience. You have to be willing to wait until the time is right. In a book on his shelf, I find these words from Simone Weil: "There is no attitude of greater humility than to wait in silence and patience...It is patience that transmutes time into eternity."

Later on that night I look for the stars, I lie in bed with my eyes closed and my mind wildly alive. It's like the night my first time on Patmos I walked through my grandparents' house, but this time it seems the whole universe is there in my mind, with wonderful things happening everywhere, in every corner, drawn from the past, the present, and even the future. Among the images that come to me are those from a night I spent with a girl when I was twenty-one. I remember every moment of our time together. While it isn't a memory of being in love, it's a memory of being fully alive, fully aware of another person. And maybe that's a memory, in its way, of love too. The images and feelings go on for what seem like hours, and when I finally fall asleep I have a feeling, while still sleeping, that all of the dreams I'm having are happy too.

It seems the next morning as if the night, with its wondrous openness to the universe, has cracked the hard shell of yesterday, allowing the joy of today and tomorrow to fill my heart. The wind is gone and the weather has warmed into the mid-sixties. When I walk the road north, where I once thought the landscape looked biblical, I feel, for the first time this visit, an unalloyed happiness. It seems I've finished the work of sifting the past and am free to experience the rest of my solitude with a light and merry heart. As I pass down the asphalt road to a place called Agriolivadi, I notice an older stone-paved road I gamboled down when I was younger. The memory adds to my joy, making me feel I have *lived* so many happy days in so many ways it's a gift to be old and have memories.

At the bottom of the road, where several whitewashed buildings cluster, sunlight bathes the empty beach. I sit down by the still sea, my back against a rock wall and a cushion I've found, and sketch a drawing for Sylvia on her birthday. Then, in a breach of my solitude, I call to wish her a happy day and we chat until the sun goes down. She asks if my trip has been worthwhile and I tell her it has, although I'll wait until I'm with her again to give her the details.

When our call is done, I cross the empty beach alone. My heart is full of solitude and relationship, Patmos and home, light and dark and the presence of beauty in everything. As I climb the hill to the main road, the sun retreats across the headlands below me and a deep contentment fills my heart. On the way into town, I walk in thickened shadows at first, but as I start the last descent a brilliant sun appears before me, blinding me with yellow light. Rounding the final corner, where the land plunges toward the sea, I notice a single boat heading slowly west. With the sun behind a hill, the sky in that direction is a lovely blend of orange glow and thin cloud in pale blue. As I watch the boat motor toward the silhouette of a thin island, I feel suddenly as if I'm on it, moving through a still sea toward a hazy destination.

As I walk the road that leads to Lax's house, the sky above a hill behind me turns a lovely shade of lilac while the clouds in front me turn saffron, backed by hues of darkened blue. When I reach Lax's porch, a single pink cloud drifts across the lighter blue above the monastery. Never have I ever seen a sky so beautiful in all directions.

Before I fall asleep that night, I remember all the times I've been inside this house with Lax and thank him for being a friend and a mentor. I thank him for being kind and engaging as well... and always delightful. In a life peppered with mistakes, one of the best things I ever did was cling to this man whose life and love were built on solitude.

My last afternoon, I walk to the beach I once called Pixie Beach and then out the road toward Grikou, gazing across the sea at a line of lit-up clouds. The beach and the sea and the clouds all feel like loved ones to me, and every step of my walk takes me across a land I seem to have known all my life. When I ask myself if I wish I had more days on Patmos, however, my answer is no. This time has given me more than I hoped for. And now I want to get back to my work and to Sylvia. I don't relish the thought of re-immersing myself in all that is America, but happily Sylvia has spent these weeks avoiding the media and being quiet too, and she feels the same way I do. Whatever comes, whatever we face, we'll go forward together—two solitudes that meet, protect, and greet each other.

Final Thoughts

Most of my views on the benefits of solitude appear in the stories on these pages. But here are a few final thoughts for this age in which we spend so much time immersed in a sea of technology, where knowing yourself and making independent decisions grows harder every day.

1. Solitude is different from simply retreating from society. Even when its main purpose is rest or recuperation, an important part is preparing yourself to return to your community more fully alive and loving.

2. It's more important now than ever to ask the question at the heart of solitude: Who am I? In a society increasingly shaped by corporate culture, where people tend to read the same highly-advertised books, watch the same highly-advertised movies, and turn to the same news sources, solitude can break the habit of thinking and acting on autopilot. It can help you discover your own thoughts, work out your own values, and choose how you live based on your unique view of the world.

3. The thoughts in this book apply to voluntary solitude rather than forced solitude, which has its own considerations and dangers. Although voluntary solitude often involves examining your

life to the point of discomfort, it should never become a negative experience. Those for whom being alone brings thoughts and images of past trauma should talk to a counselor before deciding whether solitude is the right choice.

4. Although solitude may be structured, one of its most important characteristics is freedom. It gives us a chance to live and think for a while without the strictures imposed on us by our daily lives, allowing us to discover the natural structures and values within us. It can be especially helpful during times of transition, when we have been freed from things that have defined our lives and need to know what our bedrock beliefs and values are. Having a specific place for solitude anchors us as we explore our freedom.

5. The first task in solitude is always to quiet our surface mind so a deeper mind and spirit can emerge. In this quieter space, it is easier to let what comes come without trying to control it. What we experience in solitude is not solitude itself but what choosing to be alone allows to happen inside us.

6. Just as solitude and silence enhance our ability to be fully present in an active life, an active life enhances our appreciation for solitude and silence.

7. Detaching ourselves from the technologies so deeply entwined with our daily lives allows us to have an unmediated experience of ourselves and the world around us. Detaching ourselves from our families and social groups allows us to see who we are when we aren't defined by others. The freedom to be unavailable—not on call—can begin with something as simple as turning off the notifications on your phone.

8. Solitude makes it more possible to perceive and experience our

God for ourselves rather than relying solely on images or concepts received from others.

9. Because we spend more time alone as we age and a longer life offers more of ourselves to explore, it's especially important for older people to avoid the pitfalls of loneliness by pursuing voluntary solitude on a regular basis, if they can.

10. By freeing us from thinking in conventional ways about conventional things, solitude opens the door to creativity. It's difficult to create something new or find your true direction if you never leave the mainstream.

Acknowledgments

Although this is a book about solitude, I couldn't have written it without invaluable support. The first thanks go to my mother, Doris McGregor, for giving me the freedom to spend time by myself at an early age—and taking me to the library. Next in line are the librarians who helped when I needed help and otherwise left me alone. As I always told my writing students, librarians are angels in disguise.

Other thanks go to: Robert Lax and Thomas Merton for showing me that solitude is so much more than being alone; Bjorn Alstad for his companionship that first time on Patmos; the foresighted planners of parks and fierce preservers of wilderness; the writers, thinkers, and spiritual souls who've shared their wisdom with the world; and those from every tradition and culture who continue to teach us that mystery, awe, and faith are inextricable parts of what makes life worth living.

Thank you to Gene Openshaw, who has been my companion in the pursuit of meaning for almost four decades; Father Pat Hannon, who read this manuscript with a loving but critical eye; and Jon Sweeney, who trusted for years that there was a book like this in me.

Thank you to Paul Cohen, Colin Rolfe, and the others at Monkfish Publishing who do so much to bring meaningful books into the world. Thank you for taking this project on and taking good care of it.

Thank you to Nico and Ritsa Eliou for offering Lax's house, caring for me while I was in Greece, and being such kind friends and thoughtful citizens of the world. Thank you to Marcia Kelly for showing me again and again that generosity is the gateway to abundance.

Thank you to my nieces and nephews—Katie Bassett, Michelle Farkas, Jeremy Farkas, Nicole Jones, and Emmett Hoelscher (Mr. Moak)—for giving me so many reasons to believe in the future and being such loving, joyful, and vital companions during my later days on this earth.

Finally and foremost, thank you to Sylvia, who understands and protects my solitude; shares my sorrows and joys, tears and laughter; and teaches me, day after day, what I could never learn by myself: the deepest, truest meaning of love.

About the Author

Michael N. McGregor is a Seattle-based essayist, biographer, novelist, journalist, and editor.

His first book, *Pure Act: The Uncommon Life of Robert Lax*, received an Excellence in Writing Award from the Association of Catholic Publishers and was a finalist for a Washington State Book Award, a Catholic Press Association Book Award, and the Religion Newswriters Association's Book of the Year. The *New York Times Book Review* called *Pure Act* "vivid and engaging" and the *Oregonian* described it as "deeply satisfying." The American Association of University Publishers named it one of its top ten books in American Studies for libraries.

McGregor's second book, *The Last Grand Tour*, a novel, was published by Korza Books in January 2025. In a starred review, *Kirkus Reviews* called it "a captivating exploration of the promise and burden of passionate love."

In addition to publishing dozens of shorter creative works in publications such as *Poetry*, *Tin House*, *Orion*, *Image*, and *Notre Dame Magazine*, McGregor taught creative writing for over twenty years, including seventeen at Portland State University, where he is professor emeritus. During his years at PSU, McGregor helped found the MFA in Creative Writing program and received numerous outstanding-teaching awards.

McGregor has been a guest on NPR's "Talk of the Nation" and Oregon Public Broadcasting's "Think Out Loud." He has also recorded podcast segments for *Poetry* magazine, City Lights Bookstore, Late Night Library, and Urban Roots. He hosts the Writers-in-Conversation series at the Cascadia Art Museum in Edmonds, WA, and curates the website WritingtheNorthwest. com.

You can learn more about McGregor by visiting his website: michaelnmcgregor.com.

You may also be interested in

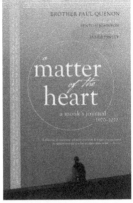

A Matter of the Heart: A Monk's Journal,
1970–2022　　　　　　　　　　**Brother Paul Quenon**

"A deep sense of contentment and peace arises from these pages that can remind the monk in every one of us how we might choose to live." —Pico Iyer

In the spirit of Thomas Merton's *The Sign of Jonas* come six decades of life at the Abbey of Gethsemani from the journal of one of Merton's former novices. Readers are introduced to the inner and outer of a monk's life. Reflections, meditations, and wanderings are mingled with experiences in nature, community, and sketches of monks—saintly, comical, or strange. Entries are arranged according to the decade they occurred in, including the visit of the Dalai Lama and other occasions when this contemplative's life has intersected with spiritual teachers outside the monastery.

You Are the Future: Living the Questions with Rainer
Maria Rilke　　　**Mark S. Burrows & Stephanie Dowrick**

A poet who can change your life.

"In Rilke, we encounter a poet who holds together what often seems at odds: youth and wisdom; focus and freedom; devotion and doubt; God and the self. With Mark S. Burrows and Stephanie Dowrick we are in the safe hands of writers who are sensitive to this exquisite tension of Rilke's vision, and who also hold it themselves.... *You Are the Future* beckons us to discover a wise way to live a life in the company of self and others."
—Pádraig Ó Tuama

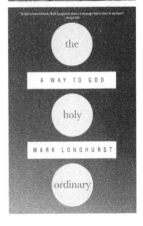

The Holy Ordinary: A Way to God　　　**Mark Longhurst**

Locates mysticism as the essential experiential center of Christian faith.

The Holy Ordinary takes its inspiration from mystics, modern prophets, and saints, with surprising insights from Christian scriptures.

"Drink from these reflections and prepare to be awakened and transformed." —**Phileena Nikole**, author of *Pilgrimage of a Soul*

"In this wonderful book, Mark Longhurst shares a message that is dear to my heart." —**Richard Rohr**

Available from Booksellers Everywhere
Monkfish Book Publishing • Rhinebeck, New York • monkfishpublishing.com